Contents

Acknowledgements

My media career has spanned two decades so far, during which I have worked with some terrific people. Thank you to the independent production companies that gave me my first break on television – Gerald Heffernan at Frontier Films, Plum Tindall at Tindall Productions and Mark Quinn at Highwire.

Thanks to the Automobile Association and AA Roadwatch for my first real job and my double-barrelled name, and especially to my friend Conor Faughnan.

Over the last decade, a large part of my life was spent with my TV family. We've shared a lot of laughs, a few tears and too many doughnuts (I miss texting from the slip road). I would like to say a big thank you to my cameramen and women, the guys on the floor (floor managers, programme directors, autocue operators, runners), my pals in the gallery (on sound, cameras and lighting, the engineers, the operators and the producers), the editors, the researchers, the make-up department (which I renamed 'Lourdes' for the miracles they perform on a daily basis), my fellow reporters and presenters and the management of TV3 for giving me the experience of a lifetime.

I am privileged to have been photographed, styled and dressed by some of the best in the business and I would like to take this opportunity to thank all the talented professionals who continue to make me feel and look the best I can be (well, them and Photoshop!).

To the press photographers (there are too many to mention), sincerely, thanks guys – no more hiding in trees though, OK? (You know who you are!) I am also grateful to the fashion and features photographers who have taken the time to make the whole 'posing' process not only painless, but enjoyable.

Thank you to the make-up artists for continuously covering my bumps and blemishes, the hair stylists for my crowning glory (you even impressed Garnier!) and to the wardrobe stylists who do all the hard work of sourcing the best styles for a shoot. They also know that I always have a preference to wear Irish, not least because it's important to champion and support homegrown talent, but also because Irish designers can hold their own amongst the best in the world. Thanks to all the wonderful Irish designers, labels, boutiques and department stores who allow me to be their clotheshorse.

Thank you to my publisher, Blackwater Press, and especially John O'Connor for reading my *Sunday World Magazine* column and believing my stories were worthy of a book. Thank you to Kristin Jensen, my editor, who was a dream to work with, and also to my designers, Liz White and Niamh Carey, the best in the business.

Thank you to my agent, Noel Kelly, for championing me and to Niamh Kirwan at NK Management, the woman neither of us could live without.

To my family, especially Dad, for encouraging me to take control of my life, and Mum, for having absolute faith in me (and for always telling me so). To my parents-in-law for being so thoughtful (and ever-ready to celebrate my smallest achievement!). A big hug to my five sisters and brother for your constant words of support and to my pal Ali for listening to my stories over the years, remembering the ones I forgot and most importantly for encouraging me to interview The Devlins very early on in my career. And on that subject – to my husband Peter, my rock. Thank you for being my best friend, my advisor, my editor, my shoulder to cry on, for making me laugh, making me believe in myself and making me endless cups of tea. For editing me (as you say yourself, I have a natural ability to make a short story long), for loving me and for giving us our *raison d'être*, Emelia and Romy. You are the kindest, most patient and genuine person I have ever known. I love you.

www.lorrainekeane.com

Dedication

This book is dedicated to Tante Lizzie (Elizabeth Rivaud) and The Breener (Fr. Sean Breen), who have given me some of my fondest memories – you are with me always – and to our little friend Ruby Ayoub, who we miss very much.

Absolute Beginner

I often wish I had the job people think I have. Don't get me wrong – having spent over a decade as entertainment correspondent and presenter of *Xposé* on TV3, I've had a wonderful time. I have also enjoyed my work as a journalist for numerous publications and have met some wonderful people along the way. But as the saying goes, it's not like it is on TV.

When students ask me what the most important aspect of my job is, I always say it's having a positive attitude. You'll get told 'no' more often than 'yes', and you can't accept no for an answer. You have to be persistent. You have to get the interview. As long as nobody gets hurt or takes offence (I've never done 'nasty'), then what's the worst that can happen? It's only show business reporting, and I for one have never taken it too seriously. Tracking down Osama Bin Laden and asking the wrong question could be life threatening, but the same cannot be said of someone like Daniel O'Donnell (although I believe some of his fans are as zealous as Al-Qaeda, so I might have to be careful). For me, the job is just a job, but I always work hard on whatever I'm working on to make it the best it can be.

Having It All?

Over the last 10 years I've watched the currency of celebrity devalue. Reality TV has created a surplus of disposable celebrities and the tabloids decide when their 15 minutes are up. More often than not, these flash-in-the-pan stars are the most difficult to deal with. The real celebrities, people like Daniel Day-Lewis, Will Smith and Bruce Springsteen, behave like gentlemen, true professionals. It's usually the *Big Brother* runner-up from last year who is sure to have more attitude. Hopefully this book will go some way to dispelling the myths behind the celebrities and the shows.

When students ask me what the most important aspect of my job is, I always say it's having a positive attitude.

I must admit to enjoying the benefits of minor celebrity status. Yes, it's great for getting a booking in a restaurant, an upgrade on a flight or tickets to a sold-out show, but the falsehood of appearing to 'have it all' did concern me. A lot of working mothers ask me how I'm able to do it and the only honest answer is that unless you can get the balance right, family life suffers. You can't work five or six 10-hour days a week and not miss out on your children's formative years. It was difficult to leave them in the morning and quite often not get back early enough in the evening to put them to bed.

'And you always manage to look so glamorous!' Yes, but that can be the most challenging part of the job. An advantage is being able to borrow clothes from designers

who are looking for exposure, plus there is a hair and make-up department. But having to do it every day – wearing something completely different and putting some degree of thought into it, usually under the pressure of getting kids ready for school – becomes monotonous and tiring after a while. When I started as entertainment correspondent I was uncompromising, obsessive and incredibly tenacious, but a combination of experience in the job and experience as a mother made me slightly more pragmatic. Having unwittingly presented a live news report with baby spew on my left shoulder, I learned not to sweat the small stuff.

Early Days at TV3

Prior to working in TV3 I had presented several shows for RTÉ (*Live at Three, RPM Motorsport, Start Me Up*) and the difference between the two stations couldn't have been greater. As a fledgling commercial station, TV3 was hugely under-resourced. Back in 1998 it was a small station with big ambitions, but such was (and still is) the enthusiasm of people with a desire to work in TV that there was no end to the amount of young talent queuing up to work for a fraction of a BBC or RTÉ salary.

As presenters, we were expected to research, write, produce, present, edit and voice-over packages. When we were sent out on a job it was as a two-man crew – the presenter and cameraman (who also drove and did the sound and lighting). This was bare bones broadcasting, and for a bottom-of-the-line commercial station, it worked. Within five years the station had turned a profit for its then owners, Canadian media giant Canwest.

Of course, TV3 is in the business of making money, not TV personalities, so a pattern developed where young talent got work experience and moved on. Over the years, TV3 has lost many of its brightest stars in the areas of presenting (Claire Byrne to Newstalk (now RTÉ), Conor McNamara to BBC Sports, Amanda Byram to Channel 4, then the US, and Gráinne Seoige to RTÉ and ITV) as well as a lot of talented producers, cameramen (and women) and directors. The on-air talent was never replaced by headhunting from other stations – it was more cost-effective to promote from within. This made for hilarious viewing at the Christmas parties, where the 'outtakes' show reel was always the highlight of the entertainment.

> *Having unwittingly presented a live news report with baby spew on my left shoulder, I learned not to sweat the small stuff.*

Here I am with the Ireland AM *team – I was covering for Amanda Byram*

Cruelly, the guys who put it together always included a few auditions by aspiring weathermen or sports reporters who fancied a change from the humdrum of the accounts or marketing departments.

The benefit of this high-pressure 'them and us' work environment led to great camaraderie among the team. My 'other family' was my TV3 family, who gave me their friendship and support over the years. The newsroom, which is basically one big open-plan office where staff from all shows work, was always buzzing and was an exciting place to be. Impossible deadlines, made worse by Dublin traffic jams, were a part of everyday life. It was difficult enough racing around town trying to get a story ready for air that evening, never mind having to look glamorous at the same time. We were all in the same boat and it bonded us together and created a great team spirit.

In the early days we enjoyed being the underdog and worked harder because of it. Ireland definitely needed another national station, and TV3 came along at the perfect time. It was on the cusp of the Celtic Tiger boom and there was a lot of good news around. The press had a field day with the launch of the 'bevy of beauties' to take on RTÉ in the ratings war. Headlines about sexual chemistry at the news desk between 'older man' Alan Cantwell and 'younger woman' Gráinne Seoige got the station a lot of free publicity, but the truth was less exciting. There was more sexual chemistry between Enda Kenny and Brian Cowen during a bank crisis debate, but we never let the truth get in the way of a good story.

Gráinne, Claire Byrne, Amanda Byram, Maura Derrane and myself were regularly wheeled out to pose for the press at various events and a national advertising campaign ensured visibility practically everywhere.

There was no shortage of content for my entertainment slot on the evening news back then. People were coming to party in Dublin and I was there to interview them. I also covered events abroad to try to meet the ever-increasing demand for showbiz news. The year after we launched, *VIP Magazine* hit the shelves and confirmed the Irish appetite for all things celebrity, no matter how minor (and yes, I include myself, cover girl no less than six times!).

> *In the early days we enjoyed being the underdog and worked harder because of it.*

On the cover of VIP Magazine

And then there was one. We organised a TV3 girls' Christmas party most years. Colette Fitzpatrick is the only one in this photo still working at the station. Pictured are (l–r)) Claire Byrne, Gráinne Seoige, Rachel Smalley, Colette, me, Maura Derrane and Deirdre Grant.

Xposé Is Launched

Over the years I made several cases to my bosses for my own entertainment show, but it wasn't until April 2007 that we finally launched *Xposé*. Critics questioned our ability to find enough content to fill a 30-minute show, five days a week, but this was at the peak of Dublin's party decade and we knew we'd have no problems. There were more launches, parties, premieres and shows per week than we knew what to do with. It took a team of four reporters (Aisling, Sybil, Lisa and Karen) to cover all the events, both nationally and globally. The show perfectly summed up the time and the place – the era of the Celtic Tiger.

There were plenty of challenges in that first decade as entertainment correspondent. In this book I hope to explain how exciting it was to meet the most talented actors, musicians, comedians, politicians, models, writers, entrepreneurs and designers. I was privileged to get to work with many amazing presenters and crews and travel to the most fantastic locations.

It wasn't all champagne and roses. There were many nightmares. I've had my fair share of disastrous interviews, where the interviewee wouldn't talk or I asked the wrong question, which in turn upset them, or maybe they were just being themselves

Xposé launch night in Dublin City Hall, with (l–r) Lisa, Aisling, Karen and Sybil

(I'd really hate to single anyone out, Mick Hucknall). I've been shouted at, pushed around, propositioned and brought to tears on many occasions – and that was before I even left the office!

But I've also had the honour of being driven around in a sports car by Paul Newman. I danced the foxtrot in a New York nightclub with Bono. I introduced Prince Charles at his first public engagement in the Republic of Ireland and dined with President Clinton while he was still in office.

Best of all, I got to meet my husband through the day job, and because I had to interview him and his band, The Devlins, our very first encounter is on DVD for our children to watch in years to come.

Starting Out

Once a year at a Keane family gathering, usually around Christmastime, one of my six siblings will inevitably shout, 'Mum, put on Lorraine's programme!'

The TV show they're referring to isn't my heartfelt Trócaire documentary, chronicling my journey to the impoverished shantytowns of Mozambique and Zimbabwe for RTÉ's *Nationwide*. Nor is it my Oscars special from LA or even my solo presentation of the TV Now Awards ceremony. No, for their amusement they like to replay the first ever 'programme' I made on a Handycam when I was still in school on the history of Rathfarnham Castle. I couldn't call it presenting, but I was walking and talking nonsense, to an unsteady camera, for the very first time. It's still the most uncomfortable, cringe-worthy, mortifying piece of 'television' I have ever had to watch. What's worse is the fact that my family make me endure it on an annual basis.

But we all have to start somewhere, and I believe that when you're starting out in an industry, particularly one as small and competitive as media, you should be willing to work for free.

While I was in Senior College Ballyfermot studying journalism and broadcasting, *The Fitzwilliam Post*, a free Dublin newspaper, took me on as their entertainment writer on the condition that I sold ads around my stories. I got paid a commission on the ad revenue I brought in (well, that was the idea), and when I look back on it, the

> *It's still the most uncomfortable, cringe-worthy, mortifying piece of 'television' I have ever had to watch.*

paper was in the win-win situation of having a journalist who doubled as a sales rep they didn't have to pay.

Kenny Rogers was my first big interview. I remember being absolutely terrified going into the press conference with my brand new journalist's notebook full of questions. Unfortunately I only got one question in, at the very end, but I had the good sense to record everyone else's so at least I had something to write about when I got back to the office.

Within a few weeks I was given an entertainment double page spread, which I was very impressed with. Unfortunately, cold calling media sales wasn't my forte, so I decided I'd earn my wages elsewhere (working for a retail chain in the evenings and at weekends) and just use the paper for practising my interview techniques and writing. They seemed happy enough to take free copy and send someone else out into the field to look after the advertising sales, and so I got my first work experience of deadlines, interviews and readers, and with it a taste for the excitement of a newsroom.

Around that time, I learned that RTÉ had a training centre, headed up by Denis Madden. I hounded the poor man until he eventually gave in and let me take part in their sessions. My idea was that if RTÉ had to train producers and directors to produce and direct, then surely they would need presenters to present for them during their training classes – a 'stand in', so to speak. Previously when they needed a guinea pig to stand in front of a camera they just used administration or technical staff working in the centre, but these people wouldn't take this at all seriously – well, not as seriously as someone like me who needed experience in front of the camera. I wanted to practise reading an autocue, etc., and I persuaded Denis that they needed someone reliable to present during their training and exams.

I worked, or should I say practised, in RTÉ's training centre every weekend, without pay, for months. During that time I assembled what I thought was useful footage for a show reel (but looking back it's amazing that I got to work in TV at all – it was appalling!) and I met some influential people, or at least people who went on to become influential, such as Noel Curran, RTÉ's last managing director of television. The next time I was to meet Noel was during my auditions/screen tests for presenter of the Eurovision in 1997, by which time he was a fully qualified and highly respected producer.

The screen tests were the most difficult of my career, as they were carried out in three languages – English, Irish and French. The fact that I didn't have a word of Irish (unless I needed to ask to use the loo during the show, though I'm not sure 'An bhfuil cead agam dul go dtí an leithreas' would have impressed any of the 50 million

I hounded the poor man until he eventually gave in and let me take part in their sessions.

global viewers) didn't deter me. Come to think of it, my French wasn't much better. I begged a friend of my parents', Irish schoolteacher Paul Dalton, to help me with my Irish grinds. Paul dutifully obliged (I will be eternally grateful) and we did a crash course in Irish during the six weeks of auditions. It obviously worked, as I managed to convince the judges I knew what I was saying and got to the final round of the last three female presenters. But experience won over brazenness in the end, and Carrie Crowley got the job alongside Ronan Keating. I was heartbroken.

I remember having to interview Carrie some weeks later as part of a weekly 'celebrity through the keyhole'-type segment I was doing for *Live at Three* with Derek Davis and Thelma Mansfield. Part of the interview followed her on a shopping trip to find her clothes and shoes for the big night. She didn't know I had gone for the same job and I didn't tell her. We became neighbours years later and laugh about it to this day. She was wonderful on the night and did us all proud.

I had no shortage of confidence then. There are many things I did in my late teens and twenties to get my foot in the door that I'd never have the nerve to do now. When you're young, you don't think about the consequences. Youth is a wonderful freedom. Nowadays I probably consider other people and other people's opinions too much. I guess when you're older there's a feeling of having more to lose.

> *There are many things I did in my late teens and twenties to get my foot in the door that I'd never have the nerve to do now.*

New Job, New Double-barrelled Name

Having lost out on what was then the dream job of the Eurovision, I continued with the day job at AA Roadwatch. I was one of four reporters from AA (Conor Faughnan, Philip Hughes and David Hughes) who were broadcasting on Radio 1. Two of us worked the morning shift and the other two did evenings/drive time. In between, as an employee of the Automobile Association, we worked in the Rescue Centre taking breakdown calls and deploying AA Patrols.

The AA had just invested a huge amount of money into marketing and research, which revealed that although the company was generally perceived positively – old, traditional and therefore reliable – they wanted to move away from the 'grey-haired man driving a Jaguar' image. They needed to reach the younger (18- to 35-year-olds) male and female market who now accounted for the majority of drivers on our roads.

AA Roadwatch was (and still is) an incredible public relations vehicle for the AA. They had established constant brand recognition at peak times on Ireland's biggest national station, Radio 1, but I felt we had to get on 2FM to reach a younger audience. Not one of the reporters was over the age of 23 at the time, so even the team portrayed a younger AA image. Unfortunately, 2FM had been offered the service in the past and had declined. I decided I would try again.

I set up a meeting with the station manager, Bill O'Donovan, under the pretence that I was the new 'boss' of AA Roadwatch. A few days later I arrived at RTÉ's radio building to discover Bill had invited the presenter of the highest-rating morning show, Ian Dempsey, and producer John Clarke to join us. If they were going to start broadcasting traffic news, Ian and John would have to be in agreement because it would be during their programme. Three against one, I felt a little out of my depth. Through a combination of blinding them with statistics and baffling them with bullshit (and maybe even a little charm), I managed to convince them to give us a month's trial. They agreed on the basis that I would do the reports, which I took as a huge compliment. I found out later that Ian and John had been looking to include a female in their show's line-up because up until then it was an all-male show – Ian presenting, Anthony Murnane on news, Des Cahill on sports. It was a case of being in the right place at the right time – and being the right gender. I was in! But it meant I would be forced to adopt the double-barrel moniker of 'Lorraine Keane, AA Roadwatch' for many years to come.

I practically skipped back to my superiors in the AA that day with the news. They were delighted. The month went well and we became a permanent part of the show. It wasn't long before Barry Lang, presenter of the evening drive time show, also took us on.

> *It was a case of being in the right place at the right time – and being the right gender.*

As a result, I was promoted to manager of AA Roadwatch, which meant that now I really was the boss! Within a year, AA Roadwatch was on 32 radio stations across the country.

The next move was to get AA Roadwatch onto television. Denis Fisk, director of AA, my boss, came up with the idea of AA Holiday Roadwatch, a bulletin that aired during the summer months to help motorists planning on travelling abroad. I was given the gig. It was my first experience of 'real' TV and I loved it. Once a week, on Thursday afternoons, I would pre-record a 90-second bulletin that was aired after the RTÉ1 *Six One News* that day. I would write the script and pick out the maps the night before and learn off the entire piece by the time I got to studio the next day, as we had no budget for an autocue – it was all shot in a small production suite near RTÉ in one take.

It was because of one of these bulletins that I got my first bona fide television presenting job. Frontier Films was producing a business show for RTÉ called *Start Me Up* with lawyer/presenter Will Leahy and footballer Niall Quinn. They offered me the co-presenting job and I couldn't have been happier. I remember reading a preview in the newspaper where they referred to Lorraine Keane, TV Presenter – I was thrilled. Following on from that came the offer of presenting *RPM Motorsport* on RTÉ and UTV and then *Drive* on RTÉ.

The producers of *Live at Three* asked me to do some filming for them and I jumped at the opportunity. I found the 'live' aspect of presenting a show exhilarating and couldn't believe it when they asked me to fill in for their anchor, Thelma Mansfield, while she was on holiday.

All of this involved some serious double-jobbing, as I was still working full time for the AA and managing Roadwatch. It was a very exciting time, but incredibly busy as well. By day I was working in the AA from 6 a.m. to 5 p.m. and by night studying PR from 6 p.m. to 10 p.m. The company was very understanding, and I worked hard at not letting the RTÉ gigs interfere with the day job. I used my holidays to film shows and spent almost every weekend and evening working. Television was like a hobby for me. I did it outside of work, in the evenings or at the weekends, but it meant my spare time and social life were non-existent. The situation was becoming more and more untenable, so when TV3 approached me to offer me the full-time position of entertainment correspondent, I jumped at the chance and relished the thought of getting my life back.

Television was like a hobby for me. I did it outside of work, in the evenings or at the weekends, but it meant my spare time and social life were non-existent.

But then I spotted my opportunity. Bono, Larry, Edge and Adam were approaching the set in a black people carrier, surrounded by an entourage of about 30 people. Uncomfortable as it was to do, I marched straight over, politely and apologetically. I knew my time would be limited and was expecting the tap on the shoulder any second, so I had to get as much information across as possible about myself and what I wanted before I was sent away.

'Hi there. I am so sorry about this, but my name is Lorraine Keane, I'm the entertainment correspondent with TV3, Ireland's new TV station, and we're going to air tonight for the first time. I would love a very quick word about...' Too late. They had looked around and had definitely seen me and may have even listened, but the security guard dragged me away before I could get any reaction or response.

Never one to give up, while I was being escorted away, I continued, getting louder: 'Please, Bono, Larry, anyone? It's my first day on air and if I go back with nothing it will be a disaster!'

By this stage I was out of sight of the band and back behind the barrier beside the head of their PR office, Lindsey Holmes (who I later came to realise is one of the best and most highly respected people in the business and who also became a great friend of mine). Lindsey marched towards me, infuriated by this new little upstart on the block. I deservedly got a bit of an earful, which I didn't really need as my pride had already taken a bruising, but despite all that I dusted myself down and started to concentrate on Plan B. There were many varied characters making cameo appearances in the music video – Boyzone, Irish boxing legend Steve Collins, an entire troupe from *Riverdance*, the Artane Boys Band, a circus, the Dublin Fire Brigade as well as Bono's wife, Ali (who the song was written about). As a back-up, I could get short comments from all of these people and edit them together to make an interesting but less impressive package. In the hour that followed I managed to get a one-on-one with everyone but Ali, and although the interviews went well, I still couldn't help feeling disappointed.

It was now almost one o'clock and I had to leave by 2 p.m. at the latest. I spotted U2 shuffling towards the people carrier once more, obviously about to leave for lunch. I ran over to Lindsey and begged. 'Please, please just ask them for me, just once? I didn't get a definite answer and if they say no I will just go, I promise.' I had a feeling that if they could, they would. I had read so much about the band in the past and they always came across as nice guys. If they had said no, then fine, but I wasn't sure if not answering me earlier was a no or just a pause before they gave someone else the chance to answer.

> *It was our first day on air – I had to prove myself and I wanted TV3 to have something the other stations didn't.*

I don't know whether it was out of pity or weariness, but Lindsey said OK. She radioed U2's people and made the request on my behalf. The answer came back – 'Maybe after lunch, when they get back.'

'But that will be too late. I have to leave, I should be gone now,' I explained. But the people carrier whizzed off and the band were gone.

Completely deflated, I gave my business card to Lindsey and thanked her for trying. The cameraman and I packed up and got into the car, and just as we were pulling out of our parking space my phone rang. It was Lindsey. 'Come back, come back. We have Larry for you. Larry has delayed his lunch to come back and talk to you.'

> *'Come back, come back. We have Larry for you. Larry has delayed his lunch to come back and talk to you.'*

I couldn't believe it. Larry, the most camera shy of the lot! He rarely does interviews and now he was missing lunch for me? I was euphoric. We whizzed back and I jumped out. The cameraman set up as I chatted to Larry and thanked him (innumerable times, I'm sure) before beginning a one-on-one interview. I had a grin from ear to ear all the way back to the studio, and to this day, every time I hear 'The Sweetest Thing' I can't help smiling. It triggers so many fond memories for me, both professionally and personally: my first live news broadcast, TV3's first day on air and the first of many wonderful memories U2 have given me over the years. They have always been and will always be the most gracious, obliging and generous celebrities I have ever met – and they're the biggest rock stars in the world.

U2 in NYC

Over the course of the next 11 years I met, interviewed and got to hang out with U2 on many wonderful occasions in Dublin, London, New York and LA. A couple of favourites spring to mind. Getting access all areas for two rooftop performances with Bono and the boys was particularly special. The first, at the Viacom (or MTV) building in New York, was actually one of the most memorable of my career.

John Fitzpatrick invited a few of us to the Big Apple for the weekend. Among the party (and I mean that in both senses of the word!) were Gerry and Morah Ryan and Claudine Farrell, who gushed enthusiastically about her big brother who had 'just got a big break in Hollywood and is going to be the next big Hollywood star – you should interview him, he's going to be huge' (of course, it was Colin she was talking about). The occasion was a fundraiser for Hilary Clinton at John Fitzpatrick's hotel during Bill Clinton's last term in office. Needless to say, we all accepted the invitation immediately. We were dying to meet the controversial President and his wife and jumped at any opportunity to spend time in New York. The city is an exhilarating place to be at any time, but with the addition of the President's entourage, the Secret Service and the press, it was like being on the set of *The West Wing* and *In the Line of Fire*!

But it was the late, great Gerry Ryan's little black book that made the weekend even more exciting. U2 just happened to be in New York that same weekend. Gerry gave them a call, and before we knew it we were on a VIP club crawl around the city with Bono, Adam, Edge and Larry.

With Hilary and Bill Clinton and John Fitzpatrick at Fitzpatrick's Hotel in New York City

There was some confusion as to where we were meeting and it had something to do with several bars in NYC with similarly abbreviated names (O2, H2O, 2, Zero). I imagine this kind of thing happens quite a lot in a city with thousands of bars. Paul McGuinness had told Bono the name of the bar but he had forgotten it. 'I don't think this is the right place,' he whispered as we walked into the dullest, quietest, most unlikely neighbourhood bar. The place just stopped dead and stared at the entourage, led by Bono, entering hesitantly and looking around. We were obviously lost and made to leave, but Bono quietly said, 'No, we're here now, let's stay for a drink.' He sensed the excitement when the half-empty premises recognised him and didn't have the heart to leave. This of course made the barmen and locals' night. Bono gladly signed autographs and posed for pictures and after a swift beer we were off again.

When we eventually met up with the rest of the band, the contrast in bars couldn't have been greater. We had gone from out-of-town suburban local to downtown celebrity hotspot. The music was loud, the crowd was beautiful and the cocktails were flowing. At one stage during the night, Bono asked me to dance with him. We did the foxtrot across the floor while the crowd parted like the Red Sea to create a large space around us so that they could take in this chance meeting with the biggest rock star in the world. Gerry Ryan, who would have had plenty of nights out with U2, looked on and was almost as thrilled by the experience as me.

It was Larry's birthday that weekend and a large cake was brought out to mark the occasion. Another excuse to continue the party!

Late into the night, Paul McGuinness asked me if I'd like to interview Bono exclusively for the show while I was there. 'Of course I would,' I replied, 'but I have

no cameraman, no equipment.' Paul assured me that wouldn't be a problem and that he, ever the gentleman, would take care of everything.

On the following Monday we were all invited to watch U2's somewhat impromptu performance on the rooftop of the Viacom building in Times Square. When we arrived (slightly late!), the band was just about to go live. We all stood back, wondering if we had time to chat. Should we wait for the lads to come to us or just wave and say hi? Not G. Ryan. He charged forward and bear hugged each band member one by one as the producers of the show looked on nervously. I'll never forget his wife Morah's teasing but totally endearing comment as we all looked on: 'Would you look at Gerard, he thinks he's in the f**king band!'

The verbal abuse continued when Gerry returned, but he took it well, as he always

With Gerry Ryan and co., Times Square, New York City

did, laughed it off and told us all where to go. He was very good at that – quick to hand out a slagging, but just as good at taking one too. We laughed so much that weekend and many times after.

As was now the norm with any 'surprise' U2 performance in any location around the world, a huge crowd was gathering below the building on Times Square. The show was *Total Request Live* and they were recording the band's short set ('Elevation', 'Beautiful Day' and 'New York') for delayed transmission two weeks later. The crowd below couldn't see very much, but they had no problem hearing the music.

U2s performance on the rooftop of the Viacom building in Times Square, New York City

Meanwhile, Paul McGuinness introduced me to my crew, a camera, sound and lighting team he had hired for me as a favour. Oh, was I going to be the best girl in the class when I got back to work!

When the band's performance ended I was chatting to Bono pre-interview and he brought me over to the edge of the rooftop, saying, 'I want to show you something very cool. On the count of three, lean over with me and look down'. He held my hand as we leaned over the wall and I experienced the most incredible adrenalin rush imaginable. Thousands of wildly ecstatic fans, filling every inch of Times Square, screamed in unison, car horns blared and cameras flashed. We pulled back and he looked at me with that knowing grin. 'Well?' I was speechless, completely blown away, and he knew it. 'Want to do it again?' he asked. Of course I did! I smiled and nodded and over we went again: complete and utter hysteria.

I had to try to compose myself and engage in some kind of coherent interview after that. I can't remember what I asked, but it didn't really matter. As usual, Bono spoke about the band, the new record and New York and it was all fantastic footage. We had exclusive shots of the performance two weeks before MTV would show it, as there was no other media with access to the rooftop.

At the end of the interview, Bono took my hand and kissed it dramatically for the cameras. It was the perfect end to the perfect weekend.

I remember how excited I was FedExing the tapes back to TV3. However, a full week later, on returning to work, I found the tapes, unused, sitting on my desk. The €100 video conversion charge (American to European format) had been deemed too expensive. The piece made it to air eventually, a day after the MTV broadcast.

> *Thousands of wildly ecstatic fans, filling every inch of Times Square, screamed in unison, car horns blared and cameras flashed.*

Closer to Home

My idea of a perfect weekend lunch is to spend it lazily at the last sitting in Cavistons seafood restaurant in Glasthule, Dublin, sipping a nice white wine before walking the coast road home.

On one such occasion the table next to ours (just me and Peter) was eventually filled by Bono, Ali and their daughters, Jordan and Eve. They obviously had the same idea, but were celebrating a joint birthday (Bono and Jordan were both born on 10 May). They kindly invited us to share some birthday cake as we chatted about the joys of parenting. It was interesting to watch Bono, the father, interact with his children. There was no difference in his animated enthusiasm for all things musical. He sang a few lines of one of the songs from Peter's band's latest album, which he said he'd brought with him on holidays and was really enjoying. His attention then turned to the music on the restaurant sound system – Stevie Wonder's 'Just Enough for the City'. He sang along for the benefit of his daughters and explained the lyrics. They gave their dad that well-worn teenage look of pity, embarrassment and amusement. Of course they know he's cool, they were just pretending to be mortified. It was sweet and endearing.

Ali Hewson is a truly amazing lady – low-key, hardworking, effortlessly stylish and incredibly beautiful. Bono once said, 'After introducing these beautiful women [supermodels] to my wife, they all lost interest in me! They're her friends now.' I can well believe it.

When the waitress brought the cake out and began a chorus of 'Happy Birthday to You', the entire restaurant (which is actually very small, with a capacity of maybe 20 people) joined in. But when it got to the name part, where all present were singing 'Happy birthday dear _____', something very strange happened. Everyone in the place knew it was Bono, but no one sang his name. This resulted in what sounded

like a bad edit of the song with just one voice singing the name 'Jordan' in that space. The voice was of course Bono's, and then everyone joined in again. Why it happened, I have no idea. Did they think they were the only ones in the restaurant who knew it was him and didn't want to give the game away? Were they doing what Dubliners do best and pretending not to notice when a superstar arrives into the room? Whatever the reason, we all thought it was funny, had a laugh and devoured the cake.

Bono and Ali were both interested in our own girls, who were at an age they obviously enjoyed with their daughters and had many questions about the stages they were at and what they were doing and saying. I sometimes forget that Ali, who is one of the most committed human rights activists, charity fundraisers and environmentalists I know, is also the most grounded and devoted mother four children could wish for.

As we got up to leave, Bono made a suggestion to me which would seemingly help attract his attention if I was ever in a media scrum situation and couldn't get through to him. He compared me to Inspector Clouseau's sidekick, Cato, who used to unexpectedly spring out at Peter Sellers in the most unusual locations. Bono explained to Ali that almost everywhere he looked, I seemed to be there with microphone in hand and camera at the ready to pounce! Bono told me all I had to do was yell 'Cato!' and he'd know I was there. I commended him on this ingenious idea and left with my Cato ace up my sleeve for future emergencies!

Hello! Hello! Cato Calling!

It wasn't long before I needed to play that ace. The lobby of U2's Clarence Hotel in Dublin was mobbed with dozens of journalists from all over the world. They were all there having heard that the band would perform songs from the *All That You Can't Leave Behind* album on the rooftop of the hotel. By the time the band arrived, the area was so overcrowded they could barely squeeze through the doors. Everyone wanted to grab a word, get a shot and of course gain access upstairs. The fact that I'm only 5'5" and slighter in build than most of my contemporaries meant that I found myself at the back of the scrum, five or six deep, swaying with the mob. Questions were being fired, cameras were flashing, security were pushing and everyone was shouting. It was manic. The band was doing their best to take control of the situation, but it was impossible to cater for everyone. I did what I always do – stuck my arm out with microphone in hand in the hope that even if I didn't get a question in I would at least pick up the audio of the band's answers. Luckily my cameraman, Alan, was over six feet tall, so he had a good chance of getting some clean shots.

Before I knew it I heard the bouncers saying, 'That's it now folks, no more questions, the band must go upstairs and perform. No journalists or cameras allowed. Principle Management will provide you with photos later.'

I couldn't believe it. Bono hadn't even seen me in the crowd and now he was being ushered away. Then it came to me.

'Cato! It's Cato, Bono! Over here!'

He stopped in the crowd, turned around and said, 'Sorry, one more question … and only from Lorraine.' Everyone looked around, a little confused and quite obviously curious. As the heads turned and followed Bono's gaze, I felt all eyes on me. I froze and it felt as though time had quite literally stood still. My heart was racing and I remember thinking, 'Jesus, what am I going to ask him now? Please, brain, give me something intelligent to say.' Five seconds felt like five minutes. My mind went blank, but I couldn't bring myself to look at my notes (it would just look so unprofessional and would waste too much time).

> *Sorry, one more question … and only from Lorraine.*

Eventually I managed to blurt out something about the switch from working with longstanding production duo Lanois and Eno to working with at least eight different producers on this latest recording. Thankfully, all eyes switched back to Bono, who smiled and even seemed pleased with the question and gave an answer that most of the journalists stayed completely silent for as they either recorded it or scribbled notes on for their story. He then gave me a wink and took the lift to the rooftop. A constant murmur returned to the lobby as the journos made calls, compared notes or headed for the bar.

Just as I had regained my composure, the lift doors opened again and the security guard beckoned to me and my cameraman. I was told that by request of the band we were invited to come watch the performance on the roof, after which Bono would give me a one-on-one interview. Another 'Beautiful Day' in my life with U2!

A Chilean Reception

I'm playing your dad in Neil Jordan's new movie,' announced Gavin Friday when I complimented him on his new look: retro sideburns and tartan flares. At first I thought he was joking, but Guggi quickly took him to task. 'Don't tell people that, Gavin,' he said, and then Bono explained to me, 'I've read the script and the character he's playing isn't exactly pleasant.'

The occasion was an award ceremony at the Chilean embassy in Dublin. The ambassador, Alberto Yoacham, was presenting Bono with the Pablo Neruda Medal of Honour in recognition of his contribution to music and to humanitarian causes, and his closest friends, artist Guggi and singer/actor Gavin Friday, were there to lend support.

The movie they were talking about was *Breakfast on Pluto*, starring Cillian Murphy and, of course, Gavin. In it, Gavin plays the part of Billy Hatchet, lead singer of a 70s glam rock band called The Mohawks. Coincidentally, my dad's show band came to prominence in 1970s Ireland as The Indians, the name they still tour under today. But that's where the similarities end. Hatchet is an aggressive gunrunning bisexual. My father, of course, is none of the above, although he does still wear war paint onstage!

I made a mental note to investigate further and let my dad know, but I was on a mission that involved trying to get some info out of Bono. Rumours were rife around town about where U2 would play their next Irish shows, but it was all speculation and nothing had been confirmed.

I got him during a quiet moment when Guggi and Gavin left for a cigarette break and half-jokingly implored him, 'Come on, Bono, you can tell me, off camera.'

He thought about it and said, 'OK. It's Croke Park.'

'What dates?'

'Can't say.'

> *Hatchet is an aggressive gunrunning bisexual. My father, of course, is none of the above, although he does still wear war paint onstage!*

It's always a pleasure being in the company of Guggi and Gavin Friday

'How many nights?'

'Three.'

'Three?' I didn't want to sound incredulous, but no one had played the new stadium before and three nights would mean a quarter of a million people. He smiled, knowing exactly what I was thinking, and nodded.

I had my exclusive!

With or Without You

Gerry Ryan RIP

That earlier wonderful weekend in New York wouldn't have happened without the irrepressible Gerry Ryan. He was so suited to the city that never sleeps and entertained us all from the moment we arrived. His friendship with U2 was a longstanding one built on trust and loyalty. On a professional level he was also very kind to other broadcasters, entertainers and campaigners.

If you needed some airtime, he'd oblige, and when he had praise he'd shout it from the rooftops. Over the years Gerry had many kind and encouraging words for me, both privately and on the airwaves. When I left TV3, I was listening to his show one morning and he was doing the newspaper front page reviews. My 'story' was on most of them and I heard him say some very flattering things, ending with the line, 'Wherever she goes next, they'll be very lucky to have her.' I never got to thank him for that before he was taken from us too soon. I wrote in my column at the time that in his memory, we should all take a leaf out of his book. Being kind, supportive, encouraging and positive can make a real difference. They say that living a life without enthusiasm is not living at all. Enthusiasm can achieve greatness and overcome apathy. Enthusiasm is something Gerry Ryan had in spades. I miss him.

·Lasting Impressions·

Quite often it can be the strangest thing or the smallest detail that makes an encounter with a person a memorable one, like making tea for Kid Rock, refusing a snog from Colin Farrell (top of my biggest regrets list!) or trying to avoid one from others. These are the stories that I shared with family over dinner or discussed at length with girlfriends on the phone. More often than not I would hear, 'It's a pity you couldn't show that on TV' or 'You should put that in a book!' They were personal encounters that usually happened off camera and were therefore never broadcast. So for my sisters and girlfriends who told me to write it all down...

Cool Hand, Warm Heart

When someone mentions 'Ol' Blue Eyes' to me, I immediately think of Paul Newman, not Frank Sinatra, as it was this striking feature that would captivate you on first meeting the screen icon. I was honoured to meet Paul Newman on two occasions and they were among the most exciting and cherished interviews of my career.

My first meeting was a nerve-wracking experience, as it had not been pre-arranged and I had to do what I hated most – doorstep.

As the founder of the Hole in the Wall Gang Camp in America, Newman had been looking for a venue to set up a European camp. The Irish government donated the Barretstown Castle estate on a 99-year lease at a cost of £1 (yes, one punt!) per year, and of course when he saw the place, the deal was done. The initial set-up, which cost in the region of $2 million, was paid for privately by Paul Newman.

Interviewing Paul Newman

I had heard that he was paying a courtesy visit to our Taoiseach at the time, Bertie Ahern, and set off for Dáil Éireann. I stood around nervously outside the government offices for two hours, and at last the doors opened and out he came. I had one brief chance to speak to him, so I made my way up the steps as quickly as possible without looking like an approaching assassin and frightening the two men away. Out of breath, with cameraman in tow, I introduced myself, apologetically, before I was actually face to face. Thankfully I had met the Taoiseach on a few previous occasions (in fact, I had introduced him at a conference just a week earlier) and he recognised me and greeted me warmly. This obviously worked in my favour, as I got the interview. I asked Newman about the charity, why he had chosen Ireland, about his enthusiasm for racing cars and his food company, Newman's Own, which donates all profits to charity (to date, in excess of $300 million). He was everything I had hoped and expected him to be – a true gentleman, one in a million.

I distinctly remember the journey back to studio. I was driving and had the tape on my passenger seat. I kept glancing down at it, so chuffed with myself and still unable to believe what had just happened. When I listened back to the interview I could hear the nervous quiver in my voice. My heart was still racing. No one else noticed, and we aired the interview that evening.

The second time I met and interviewed Paul Newman I was just as nervous, but this time because I was his passenger in a two-seater Porsche 911 speeding around a race track at 120 miles an hour – talk about surreal life experiences! His appearance then belied his 78 years – he was still fit, very handsome and his blue eyes still sparkled.

It was another promotional trip to Ireland for the charity and Porsche had donated the latest 911 model for the photo call. As we settled into the car I thought to myself, 'I'm never going to be able to hear him over the engine roar, he's so softly spoken.' As it turned out, we both just enjoyed the ride and then did the interview proper inside the building by the track.

When you're travelling that fast and someone else is driving, your natural instinct is to look at the road, just in case you see something they don't. But for me, it was difficult not to keep looking over at him and smiling like a smitten teenager. There was Butch Cassidy sitting beside me for God's sake! Cool Hand Luke was driving me around a racetrack!

When we eventually got to chat about his incredible life, the movies, his charity work and his wife and six children, he spoke in the most self-effacing manner. His marriage to actress Joanne Woodward for over 50 years is something of a legend in the entertainment world. They both shunned the Hollywood limelight, choosing instead to bring up their family in Westport, Connecticut. I told him I loved the famous quote he gave when asked how he was able to remain faithful to the same woman for so long: 'Why go out for hamburger when you can have steak at home?' He laughed and admitted, 'We're so old now that we might have to just mince the steak after all!'

Paul Newman died in September 2008 after a long battle with cancer, surrounded by family and close friends at his farmhouse home. His death was quiet, discreet and very private, just as he had lived his life. A week before his death, his daughter spoke of how they sat together in the garden admiring the beauty around them. He was taking it all in, breathing it in, and then turned to her and quietly said, 'It's been a privilege to be here.'

For me, it truly was a privilege to have met film's most enduring superstar.

> *There was Butch Cassidy sitting beside me for God's sake! Cool Hand Luke was driving me around a racetrack!*

Obsessive?
Compulsive?
Captivating!

Sometimes it's the ones you least expect that impress you the most. This was the case with Billy Bob Thornton. He was married to Angelina Jolie at the time and they were Hollywood's most popular and controversial couple. They were never out of the papers. Whether it was a story about tattooing each other's names and symbols on various parts of their bodies, wearing vials of each other's blood around their necks, her love of witchcraft, his obsessive compulsive disorder or his genuine fear of antiques, it was all very non-conformist. So when I was offered an interview with Billy Bob, I was as apprehensive as I was intrigued.

Then the demands started coming in. The interview must take place in a hotel no more than 10 years old. You have 10 minutes maximum to talk about nothing but his new album (the whole reason the normally media-shy star was doing interviews). No mention of his wife, his movies, nothing personal at all. Now I was really worried!

The interview took place in the newly renovated Clarence Hotel. I arrived early with my cameraman to set up, but Billy Bob was already inside, waiting for me. Without even a minute to look through my notes, we were told our time had started. When I walked through the door of his hotel room he was already seated on the couch, with his back to me. All I could see was the back of his head. He never stood. I walked around nervously to him to discover the reason he hadn't gotten up wasn't because he was being rude, but because he was on the phone. As soon as he saw me, he jumped up, beamed the warmest, friendliest smile and told the caller (none other than his wife, Angelina), 'We're starting now, baby, I'll call you later!' After a genuine apology, he told my now rather flustered cameraman to take his time to set up: 'We're in no rush.'

I had done my research and my opening gambit was to mention a friend and colleague of his who I had met before and was very fond of, Daniel Lanois. Daniel is U2's producer and he did the soundtrack for the brilliant *Sling Blade* movie, written by and starring Thornton. (Incidentally, in *Sling Blade*, the character Doyle Hargreaves, played by Dwight Yokam, has a phobia of antiques, while in *Monster's Ball*, Thornton's character, Hank Grotowski, insists on eating with a plastic spoon rather than using 'old silverware'.) I often found that having some sort of personal connection or reference helps to break the ice with potentially difficult interviewees. I'm not sure I needed to disarm him, but I felt comfortable enough to ask him the questions his people had told me not to and he seemed quite content to answer them. The interview ended up being one of the most relaxed and enjoyable I've ever done and our 10 minutes became 30. When 'his people' came in to tell us to wind things up, he politely told them to go away.

He was honest, open and approachable, so much so that at one stage I lifted up the small vial from around his neck and asked, 'Is this really it, Billy? Is this the vial of Angelina's blood?' He laughed and said yes.

'Is that not weird?' I asked.

'Maybe, but it keeps the press away from the important stuff to do with our relationship. Give the press a few freaky details and that's all they'll concentrate on. We can keep the really important stuff about our relationship private that way.' Genius. They were manipulating the media and taking control.

I asked him about his phobia of antiques and he told me that he just prefers new things. He doesn't like the idea of sleeping in a bed that someone might have died in (fair point) and he likes contemporary furniture and decor anyway.

For someone who had initially scared the life out of me, Billy Bob turned out to be a complete gentleman. He was also very charismatic, but naturally so. It was effortless, like he had an aura around him. It was a calming influence I had never felt from anyone else I interviewed (although Bono, Bill Clinton, Gay Byrne and the late Charles Haughey each had their own unique presence). I could see exactly why Angelina, 20 years his junior, had fallen for him. If I'm totally honest, I kind of fell for him myself.

Other interviewers haven't been as fortunate. His now-infamous blow-up on CBC in Canada is the most excruciating piece of television I've ever seen. The interviewer made reference to Billy Bob's acting career during the intro to his band, who were there to talk about their music, and as a result he answered every question with the line 'I don't know what you mean' before berating the interviewer for not treating him with respect.

My only disappointment was being able to run a mere two minutes of the 30-minute interview on the news that night, which usually equated to about two questions. One of the daily frustrations I had to endure was cutting my interviews to shreds. In this instance – and the only reason I got the interview in the first place – one of the questions had to be about the new album. His movie career was the second topic. Angelina wasn't as high profile then as she is now, which meant the audience didn't get a chance to hear about the vial of blood or their relationship with the media and each other. Quite often, the best bits ended up on the cutting room floor.

" Is this really it, Billy? Is this the vial of Angelina's blood? "

Well Hello, Dolly!

I was on holidays the week the queen of country music came to town, but I interrupted my time off and flew home to do the interview. I'm a fan and have been to her shows, so I didn't want to pass up an opportunity to meet such an amazing entertainer.

I have to say it was well worth it. The small but perfectly formed superstar (32E bust, 22-inch waist and 5 feet tall) really does have a personality befitting a showbiz legend. When she arrived, this tiny little lady practically filled the room with her warmth and charm. She was also very gracious and spoke about all aspects of her career and personal life. Married to the same man, Carl Dean Thomas, for over 40 years, she explained that they met at the Wishy-Washy Laundromat on her first day in Nashville. His very first words to her were, 'Y'all gonna get sunburnt out there, little lady.' She was 18 years old at the time. Carl has never favoured the limelight. I asked her if he had come to Ireland with her, but she said that he rarely travels with her on tour and likes to stay at home, running his asphalt business.

She spoke about her upbringing (she was the fourth of 12 children) and the difficulties her parents faced raising a family in extreme poverty ('We were dirt poor') in Tennessee during the 1940s and 1950s, living in a one-room cabin. Her success enabled her to raise some of her younger siblings, together with Carl, in their home in Nashville.

When you compare her achievements in music to the artists of today, it really is staggering what she has accomplished in her career. Dolly Parton has had 25 number one hits and a record 41 top 10 country albums, which equates to almost one album a year in her four and a half decades of making music.

But the burning question for me was how she hasn't aged a day in the last 20 years. Not wanting to insult this lovely lady, I skirted around the issue of cosmetic surgery, enhancements and her overall appearance (she was about 60 at the time), but I was intrigued and I knew the viewers would be too.

'How do manage to maintain such a wonderful, youthful appearance?' I asked in the nicest way possible.

'Well, honey,' she replied with a smile, 'it takes a lot of money to look this cheap.'

'But have you really spent a lot of money on your appearance?'

'Of course! Why should I look like an old barnyard if I don't have to?' She went on to tell me that between the wigs and the make-up, it took her at least two hours to get ready every day. How refreshingly honest!

> *Not wanting to insult this lovely lady, I skirted around the issue of cosmetic surgery, enhancements and her overall appearance.*

The following year, I saw her on *The Oprah Winfrey Show*. Oprah went one step further, enquiring as to what kind of cosmetic surgery she'd had done.

'If I see something sagging, bagging and dragging, I'm going to nip it, tuck it and suck it,' she said. She also jokingly admitted, 'If I have one more facelift, I'll have a beard!'

Towards the end of our interview, I gave her a present of my husband's band's latest CD. The Devlins had played at one of the many theatres in the Dollywood theme park (think Disneyland with a lot of country music). I'm not sure why they ended up there – maybe their booking agent made a mistake – but they seemed to enjoy it. Anyway, Dolly gushed enthusiastically about the band, saying she remembered them playing, and thanked me sincerely for the gift.

I'm not sure if she did actually remember them, but I told Peter at the time that I wouldn't be surprised if she ended up recording a cover version of one of their songs. Unfortunately, we're still 'waiting'!

When Love Came to Town

High-profile charity balls used to happen every other weekend in Dublin, but to host a €500-a-ticket night in the depths of a recession needed a real A-lister to fill the ballroom. Hollywood stars don't shine much brighter than Samuel L. Jackson, and on Valentine's night 2010 he hosted a Night for Love ball in aid of Irish Autism Action. I met him on a couple of occasions that weekend and can clearly see why men want to be him and women want to be with him.

Keith Duffy was the driving force behind the event and convinced Sam to spend the weekend in Dublin with the promise of a few rounds of golf. On his way to collect Sam from his hotel, he met a mutual friend.

'What's in the box, Keith?' enquired the friend.

'A bottle of the finest vintage Irish whiskey for Samuel L. Jackson.'

'You know he's an ex-addict who's been to rehab, don't you?'

Keith proceeded to scour the neighbouring shops, looking for something more appropriate. It had to be something novel, something the American actor wouldn't already have and it would, of course, have to be Irish. He went into Kilkenny Design and bought a chunky white Aran knit jumper.

Later that night at the ball, I heard that Sam loved it so much he'd put it on straight away and announced, 'Look, I could be Ireland's first pimp.'

I'm happy to say he didn't wear it on the night, but opted for a more appropriate black suit. He was relaxed and spoke at length about the many and varied charities he does work for, but that this event was made special not just because of the incredible entertainment (Dionne Warwick performed), but because it had given him an opportunity to play the K Club with some friends (Ronan Keating had brought him out earlier that day).

He was generous with his time, not only in conversation, but as an auction item on the night. Flights to LA, hotel accommodation and a round of golf with him raised €50,000. Two wealthy businessmen chased the prize, cheered on by a wildly enthusiastic crowd. When the hammer fell, Sam announced he would offer a second weekend to the underbidder for the same price.

The fact that Jackson didn't enjoy major movie success until he was 40 must be one of the reasons why he's so grounded. What you see is what you get – there are no airs and graces. He regularly jokes about his performance in *Snakes on a Plane* (a terrible horror movie that was panned by the critics) and being mistaken for Laurence Fishburne.

'People shout at me, "Hey, loved *The Matrix*, man!" Yeah, me too. I was on a plane and this guy sat down next to me. Finally he said something to me, and we started talking about *Pulp Fiction*. He couldn't remember the actor's name, so I tried to help and said, "I think it might have been Samuel Jackson." He jumped in, "No, no, it's the other guy, that Fishburne guy." We rode the whole flight having that conversation and then, right at the end, he looked hard at me and said, "You sure look familiar. You're sure you're not Laurence Fishburne?" I said, "No, and I definitely am not in *Pulp Fiction* either." '

As the night wore on and the calls from the guests for him to recite a few lines from *Pulp Fiction* got louder ('I get asked to do that Ezekiel speech about three times a week'), he obliged autograph and photograph hunters, but there was no mention of a 'Royale with cheese'. After Dionne Warwick's virtuoso performance, he made a quiet exit, stopping on his way out to say goodnight. As a leading man, his characters are usually bad guys, but Samuel L. Jackson, loyal husband and devoted father, is anything but.

> " *Sam loved it so much he put it on straight away and announced, 'Look, I could be Ireland's first pimp!'* "

Getting the Good Side

On occasion I was asked to supply a TV monitor for an interviewee. This allows them to view a screen before, during and after their interview to ensure they're looking their best. It was a real nuisance, since we didn't have many monitors in TV3, but when we were asked we dutifully obliged because if the request is made and we show up without a monitor, it means the interview won't happen. Bryan Adams was one such celebrity and probably the most insistent. Bryan's people even went to the trouble of sending a shot list of 'do's and don'ts' weeks before the interview:

1. Don't film the right side of his face, all shots to be taken from his left.

2. Don't go closer than a mid shot (waist up).

3. Do have a filter on the lens.

Myself and the guys in the studio used to jokingly refer to this filter as 'the beauty button'. I had one in studio for *Xposé*, but unfortunately the budget only stretched to equip one of the three cameras with it, so it defeated the purpose. Depending on which camera I was presenting to at any given time, my look went from soft focus and flattering, like Joan Collins in *Dynasty*, to harsh and unforgiving, like a barmaid in *Corrie*.

Bryan Adams's people were meticulous. They met us in the Merrion Hotel half an hour before our interview time. They had to check the shot, make changes, check it again and tweak it some more until they were finally happy. Then they called him. The funniest part was that when he arrived, he never checked the shot once himself – another case of the management having a bigger ego than the celebrity or just trying to justify their jobs. Or it could have been a case of good cop/bad cop, allowing Bryan to make the demands through his people but come across as the easygoing nice guy.

Whoever it came from, the interview with Bryan was anything but difficult; in fact, he was quite charming. Did all the fuss over the monitor make a difference? Well, actually, I have to say it did. Looking back at the footage, I must admit he was definitely more attractive on his good side, through the filter. Never underestimate the power of the beauty button!

What Happens in Vegas...

Generally I'm good at withholding judgement until I meet someone. I know it's hard not to let your preconceived notions influence how you react when meeting people for the first time, especially in such a small world where people love to talk, text and tweet incessantly about celebrities and their character flaws. In the case of Michael Flatley, I hadn't expected him to be so pleasant, a 'gentle' man in the true sense of the word, soft-spoken and gracious. It's obvious that he's not lacking in self-confidence, but even off-stage he's self-assured and at ease. Maybe it's the close Irish family upbringing or the knowledge of being the best you can possibly be in your career, but I'd say it's a combination of both (plus the fact that his bank balance reads something like $750 million).

I was invited on a press trip to Las Vegas to cover the opening of Flatley's *Lord of the Dance* show at the five-star Venetian Hotel. He had just signed a deal worth $250 million, so as you can imagine with a show that size, no expense was spared. I was the only Irish TV show there, but there were several print journalists on the junket too.

It was my first trip to the entertainment capital of the world, so I wasn't daunted by the 48-hour, eight airport stop-off round trip (OK, so not *every* expense was spared). Even the fact that I had to do all of this over a three-day period (basically 24 hours in Vegas) didn't dampen my enthusiasm.

By the time we arrived, having been in Dublin, London, Amsterdam and New York that day, it was a little disorienting to walk from Las Vegas, Nevada into what looked like the Grand Canal in Venice. The hotel was an incredible reconstruction of the Italian city, complete with indoor canals, gondolas and a ceiling designed with such clever lighting and

murals of clouds that it always feels like daytime (it's also to encourage gambling, as it's never time to go to bed).

The accommodation was too good for the measly few hours I would get to spend sleeping in it. My suite was the size of a three-bed semi, with a living room, dining area, bathroom complete with jacuzzi and a super king-size bedroom with panoramic views. I barely had time to brush my teeth before I was escorted to Flatley's suite – and I'd thought mine was impressive! Just multiply everything mine was by ten.

His personal assistant, Thomas, welcomed us and showed us where to set up. I wasn't able to bring my own crew (another expense spared, but that's it, I tell you, champagne all the way from here on in), so I hired a local cameraman, whom I had met for the first time just minutes earlier.

'I'm going to be the new King of Las Vegas!'

Flatley, dressed in an immaculate designer navy blue suit, crisp white shirt and colourfully co-ordinated tie, greeted me in a way that made me feel like I was enjoying an audience with royalty. He gestured for me to take a look out of his floor-to-ceiling windows and declared, 'I'm going to be the new King of Las Vegas!' There was a vacant plot of land not far from the Venetian that Michael told me he wanted to buy and develop: 'The first Irish casino.'

I couldn't help thinking to myself that it would never work. In Vegas, casinos give free alcohol. If you opened an Irish casino, it would be like running a free bar in Rosie O'Grady's on St Patrick's Day. But of course I didn't say that. I managed a nod and said something like, 'Great idea, makes perfect sense, Michael!'

Then we sat down and began the interview and he explained exactly what was going on. The five-year plan was that his Las Vegas show alone would be seen by over 40 million people every year – two shows a night, six nights a week for five years. That's a lot of ticket sales. He also told me that in the previous two years the *Lord of the Dance* show had premiered in Japan, Beirut, Russia, Bulgaria, South America and Africa. The show is kept on the road by three touring troupes, each with a cast of 40 dancers who were continually travelling Europe, Australia and the US.

But Michael wanted to stress that despite the millions of dollars that kept rolling in, his feet were firmly on the ground and none of it had gone to his head.

'After the show opens tonight I'm flying back to Chicago to see my parents, Michael and Eilish,' he said, who were then 74 and 66, respectively. Michael's parents hail from Sligo and Carlow and emigrated to Chicago in 1947. His father set up a successful construction business, where Michael worked as a young man, but all along knew that it was dancing he wanted to pursue. He told the story in a way that rivalled the *Billy Elliot* movie. Both parents encouraged him to follow his dream. His heritage is incredibly important to him and he's extremely proud to be Irish and to be able to share some of our culture with the world. His enthusiasm was contagious. I found myself leaving the interview humming the *Riverdance* melody – wrong tune, I know, but who can remember the theme tune to *Lord of the Dance*?

I then headed out to the desert to film a few pieces to camera, after which I left local cameraman John to shoot some general 'night-time in the city' shots while I raced back to my own Little Italy to get ready for the red carpet event.

The opening night was as over the top as expected. Billed as 'The World's Greatest Dance Show', they certainly didn't hold back on the production, and as a spectacle, it was fantastic. As a future money-making venture on the Vegas strip it was a no-brainer and the mood at the after-show party was as buoyant and boisterous as Sin City itself. Champagne, cocktails and platters of sumptuous food were on offer everywhere you turned. A DJ entertained the VIP guest list and the star of the show mingled, chatted and seemed very happy with the whole night. Being an ex-boxer, Flatley is obviously a sports fanatic, as I was introduced to many famous boxers, golfers, jockeys, snooker players and footballers as well as entertainers from Ireland and various parts of the US.

At one stage Michael approached me and asked me to dance. Thankfully, the DJ was playing dance music, not traditional Irish, so I didn't have to worry about trying to remember 'hop to knee, count two three'. I agreed, but as I was just about to find my almost as embarrassing 80s Madonna groove, he tried to get me to waltz. My waltzing skills are limited, to say the least, but I can get away with it if I lead, otherwise my dance partner risks life and limb. The thought of me doing serious damage to the world's most valuable feet (rumoured to be insured for $40 million at the time) made me panic. Despite my feeble protests and lame excuses, he launched me into some kind of waltz that I dismally tried to keep up with. Of course, the entire party was now looking on and must have thought I'd gotten too much sun that day, as my complexion had reddened to a most unattractive degree.

> *I couldn't help thinking to myself that it would never work. In Vegas, casinos give free alcohol. If you opened an Irish casino, it would be like running a free bar in Rosie O'Grady's on St Patrick's Day.*

When the longest dance in history (for me, anyway) finally ended, Michael invited me to the casino. I accepted (it was Vegas, it was my first visit, I had to gamble for God's sake!), I was flattered, but I was obviously also delusional (can I blame the oxygen being pumped through the air con? The jetlag? Even the copious amounts of cocktails?) because as we entered the casino and heads turned, I pictured myself on the set of a James Bond movie. I played the part of Lady Luck, kissing the dice for my wealthy acquaintance who would have a million dollars riding on the throw. Of course I would roll a lucky seven, win, and as a generous and sporting gesture he would split the takings with me. But when we took our seats, my dreams were shot down in flames – 'I don't gamble,' Michael said.

'What do you mean, you don't gamble?' (I'd already spent my fictitious $500,000 winnings!) 'Why not?'

'Because I have too much to lose,' came the reply.

> *It was 4 a.m. I was broke. It was time for bed.*

Well, I didn't. I watched my first $100 disappear down the hole of the dealer's table, along with my *Casino Royale* fantasy. Thirty minutes later, I was down another $100. I looked at my watch (you'll never see a clock in a casino). It was 4 a.m. I was broke. It was time for bed.

I declined the offer of a nightcap in the penthouse and with a flight of foot that would rival Flatley's 35 taps per second, I raced to my room and grabbed three hours' sleep before I had to get up, pack and begin the long journey home.

The Trouble with Simon

Just like the 13 million-plus viewers across the UK and Ireland, I've been an avid follower of *X Factor* since it first aired in 2004. I have also had many opportunities to meet its maker, Simon Cowell, thanks to Louis Walsh, but the first time I met him on his home turf was an altogether different experience.

I had flown to London for an *X Factor* Final press conference and an interview with Fergie (of the Black Eyed Peas, not the duchess). The first interview delayed me, so I arrived half an hour late to the *X Factor* studio, having changed my outfit in the back of a London cab en route (I didn't want to wear the same clothes in what would be aired as two completely separate stories). It was a big story and I was very stressed at the prospect of missing it. I rushed into the reception area and explained who I was and what had happened, only to be dismissed by a rather dour lady behind the desk. 'Number one, your name is not down on the list so you're not getting in, and two, it's nearly over now anyway and you can't disturb a press conference mid-flow.'

As with most Louis Walsh arrangements, it was verbal, not really official, and sealed with a 'Just give me a shout when you arrive'. I explained this to the woman with no personality, but she wasn't warming to me. As a last resort, I took out my mobile phone, brandishing it like some sort of weapon that was just about to inflict pain.

'Right, you've left me no option but to ring Louis on his mobile phone. He told me only to call if it was a real emergency, and I think this could be it. Now, we both know he's in the middle of a press conference and the last thing he or Simon Cowell wants right now is for a phone to ring while they're talking, and when they find out why it's ringing and whose fault it is, then you'll have to explain, not me.' It worked.

'Eh, OK then, you can go up, but try to be quiet when you're walking in.'

A security man accompanied us in the lift and we quietly snuck into a large studio filled with the British media. Louis spotted me and threw me a bemused look, as if to say, 'Late? What are you thinking?' I would have to explain later.

It seemed that the press conference was indeed drawing to a close. Simon was holding court, completely at ease and enjoying the friendly banter with the journalists. He knew most of them by name and was definitely at home, among friends, colleagues and fellow presenters. After the last question I barged through the crowd and made

> *As with most Louis Walsh arrangements, it was verbal, not really official, and sealed with a 'Just give me a shout when you arrive'.*

my way to the stage. The judges (Simon, Louis and Cheryl Cole) were being ushered into a private room off the side of the stage.

In my best fishwife bellow, I called to Louis to wait: 'And Cheryl and Simon,' I added optimistically as I got closer (Danni wasn't there, as she didn't have an act in the final). Cheryl stopped, more out of curiosity, I think, but when she saw my microphone and camera she declined the interview. Later, I managed to talk to her off camera when she approached me to admire my military waistcoat and enquire where I had bought it. Knowing I was a friend of Louis's, she teased him about his acts and about some comments he had made earlier at the press conference. She is as beautiful close up and in person as she is on television and is surprisingly petite. I was impressed by how engaging she was and enjoyed talking fashion, music and fellow judges with her.

I spoke to Louis on-camera for the show, but I really needed an interview with the main man to make the story impressive. I explained this to Louis, who dragged Simon away from a media scrum that had developed at the entrance to their private room and brought him to me. They were great together, a real double act who obviously enjoy each other's company and enjoy working together. There were a few gentle digs about the quality of their acts and the mood was so upbeat that I decided I could probably get away with asking a question about a story that was all over the British and Irish press at the time. It had been rumoured that if you were to be involved in X Factor in any capacity (contestant, guest, production staff, judge) that you first had to sign a contract of agreement – the agreement being you would only say nice things about Simon at all times.

He seemed a little taken aback. None of the other journos had asked him about it, but he said that unfortunately it was true, but that he'd had no prior knowledge of it. Apparently his lawyers had included it in the standard non-disclosure contract without informing him.

With a grin and a glance at Louis, I said, 'Doesn't it make you really sad, as in pathetic?'

Louis let out a nervous snigger, but Simon took it very well. 'Now that I know about it, I rather like it.'

'So will you be leaving it in?'

'Absolutely.'

He then turned to Louis and with a cheeky grin said, 'This one's trouble, Louis. I know trouble when I see it, and this one is definitely trouble.' He was quickly distracted by one of his assistants who finally escorted him out of the main room and I had to make do with finishing the interview talking to just Louis, which is always a pleasure.

> 'This one's trouble, Louis. I know trouble when I see it, and this one is definitely trouble.'

From Heartbreaker to Icebreaker

I first met Colin Farrell over 20 years ago, or so he says. The reason I have to take his word for it is because I honestly cannot remember. Imagine forgetting your first encounter with one of the world's biggest heartthrobs! But a scruffy 10-year-old swinging out of a tree is hardly heartthrob material. Oh, if only I knew then what I know now.

You see, Colin's best mate was a boy called Jarlath Mullahy, and his dad was the drummer in my dad's band, The Indians, for 30 years (are you still with me?). They lived in Castleknock, and seemingly my dad brought myself and my older sister to the Mullahys' house for a visit once and Colin was there, hanging out of the trees.

So close I'm blushing!

Fast forward 20-plus years and I'm on my way to interview Hollywood's hottest newcomer about his part in *Hart's War*, a World War II drama also starring Bruce Willis (in my completely biased opinion, Colin stole the show and deservedly won a Golden Globe for his performance).

I had been warned that he was likely to be a bit of a challenge – very cheeky and prone to using colourful language on-camera – so I was a little anxious. However, as soon as Colin saw me enter the room, he rushed over, gave me a big hug and gushed enthusiastically about my family, my dad's band and his friend Jarlath and explained that they'd both had a crush on me and my sisters. He was friendly and endearing and didn't swear once. He was also, in case you needed to be told, drop dead gorgeous.

Before the interview, when I asked him for a photo (for a column I was writing for *VIP Magazine* at the time), he stood so close to me that I felt myself blushing. I defy any woman to stand that close to Colin Farrell and not be overwhelmed.

Just as I was settling down to begin the interview, he asked me if I was nervous (I was starting to see his cheeky side!). His comment made matters worse, so I had to come clean.

'Yes, actually, I am. *You* make me nervous.'

I first met Colin Farrell over 20 years ago, or so he says. The reason I have to take his word for it is because I honestly cannot remember.

Then he did something I really hadn't expected – he offered to snog me! I nearly fell over.

'I reckon if we snog, it would break the ice and take your mind off being nervous. Then we can just get on with the interview.'

I have to admit that he had a point. Kissing Colin Farrell would most likely take my mind off just about anything. However, a press junket in a hotel conference room surrounded by a five-man film and production crew isn't exactly the most romantic setting. Damn it, why am I ever the romantic? Nevertheless, his suggestion did make me laugh and went some way to assuaging my nerves. The interview was relaxed, informal and fun, despite my earlier refusal of his considerate, selfless offer!

We've met lots of times since: at the *Alexander the Great* movie premiere, on the set of *Transmission*, at promo events for *Phone Booth* and *In Bruges* and at the Jameson Dublin Film Festival. We've even presented awards at the Irish Film and Television Awards together, and each and every time we've had have a laugh about it. Just a laugh, no nerves – and sadly, no snogging!

The End of the Affair

He had stopped talking and I was smiling like a teenage debutante on a date with her dreamboat.

The first time I met Ralph Fiennes, he was doing the promotional tour for Neil Jordan's film *The End of the Affair*. Fiennes was still enjoying the phenomenal success of *Schindler's List* and *The English Patient* (he was nominated for Academy Awards and Golden Globes for both and won the Best Supporting Actor BAFTA for *Schindler's List*). I had watched a preview screening of his latest work and loved it and was sure he'd be picking up a few more nominations following its release. In *The End of the Affair*, he plays the part of a passionate, jealous, spurned lover who rekindles an obsession with his ex-mistress, played brilliantly by Julianne Moore. I couldn't help feeling a twinge of jealousy watching the steamy love scenes, but tried desperately not to think of that as I approached the room where the interview was to take place.

Normally in these junket interview situations you are face to face, with a camera behind each chair focusing on the face opposite. Most actors like to keep a distance between you and them – at least six or eight feet – and sometimes they won't even get up to shake hands, they just say hello.

The set-up for this interview was quite different. There was a small two-seater couch, which meant we were very close and very cosy. Of course, I was extremely happy with this arrangement and settled into the interview straight away. As he began answering the questions, I found his voice to be incredibly hypnotic. Without realising it, I was falling into a trance, nodding wide-eyed at everything he was saying but not taking anything in (unprofessional, I admit, but it hasn't happened very often). There was a long silence. He had stopped talking and I was smiling like a teenage debutante on a date with her dreamboat. I had forgotten what I had asked him and I had no idea what he had just said or what my next question was going to be. He realised I was lost. Suddenly I was aware of his thigh pressing against mine as he leaned over and kissed me softly on the lips.

OK, that last bit didn't actually happen (but it will in the movie version of this book!). What did happen is that I stuttered and stumbled through my next question as he waited patiently with a knowing grin on his face. It was difficult to concentrate for the rest of the interview, and when it was over I left feeling slightly embarrassed but nonetheless smitten.

The next time we met he was kind enough not to mention it and I was kind enough not to mention his liaison with a blonde flight attendant in the toilet of a Qantas plane during a flight from Sydney to Mumbai. Did someone say 'passion, jealousy, spurned lover, obsession'? It was definitely the end of the affair for me!

With the hypnotic Ralph Fiennes

of the guests had partaken of the champagne and cocktails, and what little of my performance they remember is through sparkling rosé-tinted glasses.

This story served as a good icebreaker when I met Simon Le Bon a few years later. Duran Duran were starting a comeback tour (though they maintain they never really broke up, just rotated a few band members) having had a huge worldwide hit with the brilliant 'Ordinary World'. They did what many UK acts do and chose Dublin as the location for the first date on the tour. Of course they all say it's because they love the Irish fans so much, but I have a sneaking suspicion that really it's just because they can treat the show as a dress rehearsal and make any mistakes before getting to cities like London.

I was shown to the band's dressing room backstage at the Point Depot, where I was due to meet Simon for a quick interview before the gig. The tour manager left the room, and as my cameraman was setting up, I decided to have a nose around. You can find out a lot about a band by looking at their rider (list of requirements for the dressing room). The table in Simon's room was very healthy: all low-fat food, fresh sushi, crudités, low-calorie drinks and mineral water. Next door was like a vegan restaurant and the dressing room next to that had nothing but junk food – hamburgers, hot dogs, chicken kebabs, beer, Coke and crisps. Without touching a morsel (I was starving, as I had come straight from work), I got back to the area where my cameraman had set up in Simon's room and waited for him to arrive.

Paul Young (centre) with Gerald Kean (r) and one of Paul's band members

Reminiscing about Gerald and Clodagh's party worked a treat. By the time the camera was ready to roll, we were like two long-lost friends reunited. Simon asked the cameraman if he could have a look at the shot, which I thought was a bit strange, but he was probably just being professional, as it had happened a few times before. He was happy (phew!) and off we went.

Everything was going great. He was open and honest and forthcoming until about halfway through one of my questions. As the cameraman moved position, Simon leapt from his seat, shouting, 'No, no, you can't move around like that!'

My cameraman was stunned and more than a little confused. 'Why not?' he asked.

'What do you mean, why not? We agreed on a camera angle. We agreed on the shot. Why are you moving?'

I tried to mediate. 'What's the problem, Simon?'

'It's the angle. I don't want to be shot at a bad angle. Can we stick to what we agreed? No moving around, OK?'

I couldn't believe it. Here was Simon Le Bon, pop superstar, who has sold over 100 million records, and the UK tabloid press had turned him into a paranoid, insecure, fat kid. For the record, I hadn't seen him look that good in a long time – all that sushi and health food was obviously paying off. I told him as much, but all he could say was, 'Oh, and don't film the sushi, the press love that!'

I had filmed the riders but respected his request and edited it out of the final package. I also left out Simon's mini-meltdown (the cameras had been rolling for all of it). No matter how successful or content some may seem to be, even celebrities have insecurities after all.

> *I couldn't believe it. Here was Simon Le Bon, pop superstar, who has sold over 100 million records, and the UK tabloid press had turned him into a paranoid, insecure, fat kid.*

Simon and Yasmin with Ronan and Yvonne Keating

The Skinny on Victoria

In late 2001, Victoria Beckham came to Dublin to promote her eponymous debut album. Virgin Records had spent a lot of money on the album (somewhere in the region of £5 million) and the early reviews weren't good. Her first two singles had been pipped to the number one spot (by Sophie Ellis-Bextor and Kylie) and she was desperate to make this record a success. On two earlier occasions I had enjoyed talking to Emma Bunton and Mel B, but was really looking forward to meeting the most stylish former member of the Spice Girls, aka Posh Spice.

Par for the course, I received a list of 'what nots' from the record company. It basically said I could ask her anything about the new record, but nothing else.

Everyone knew the album was a turkey (it went on to sell less than 50,000 copies, which would have recouped only a fraction of the costs involved), so I had a feeling the interview might end up sounding as vacuous as her music. Despite all of this, I went along with an open mind and have to admit I was pleasantly surprised.

As the cameraman was setting up she chatted openly and enthusiastically, admiring what I was wearing (a Macari/Brennan corset and jeans), asking me who did my nails, where she should shop while she was in Dublin for the weekend and if I had any kids – all the normal girly things. It was like she was easing herself into the interview, which is usually the job of the interviewer, not the interviewee. I remember thinking, this girl has something special, a natural affability and readiness to poke fun at herself. She was actually very witty and we enjoyed a few laughs before the interview proper began. By that time, I felt I'd known her an age.

I asked the obligatory album questions, but after going through the motions I felt comfortable enough to delve a little further. She spoke honestly about being married to David – 'the love of my life' – and about having children (they had Brooklyn at the time). She discussed the difficulties of living life constantly in the spotlight: 'Sometimes we find it really hard, but we keep it as normal as we can.'

I had been told (mostly by the girls in the office) to ask about her weight. There had been a lot of controversy around that time of her ever-decreasing waistline and unhealthily skinny appearance. She didn't seem the slightest bit put out.

'I don't diet. I'm a healthy eater.'

'Do you starve yourself to stay that thin?' I asked. At a guess, I would say she has a 23-inch waist.

'No. It really annoys me that people think that. I have a little boy to look after. I don't have a nanny. I wouldn't have the energy for him if I starved myself.'

I believed her. I wanted to.

When the interview was over, I promised her a Macari/Brennan corset (I knew the design duo would be delighted), packed up and we said our goodbyes. No sooner had we left than my cameraman realised he had forgotten one of his lights. He went back to the room to get it just as Victoria's lunch was being delivered – a plate of steamed cauliflower and broccoli, no butter, no salt, just a glass of water on the side. I remember feeling like such a mug. I had been completely taken in by her. But looking back, what did I expect? The girl had hips the width of a nine-year-old boy, and you don't get to look like that from eating burgers!

I wanted to like Victoria, and I must admit that dietary habits aside, I do. She wasn't at all what I expected, having been bombarded over the years with images of the unsmiling, perfectly groomed, perfectly poised celebrity in 5-inch Louboutin heels, big sunglasses and Hermès bags. The girl I met was friendly, down to earth and very funny, if just a little bit economical with the truth.

Victoria's lunch was being delivered – a plate of steamed cauliflower and broccoli, no butter, no salt, just a glass of water on the side.

Daddy's Girl

I was talking families with the inimitable Jon Voight. He was the doting father, explaining that his daughter, unknown aspiring actress Angelina Jolie, was 'about to hit the big time with her first movie roll. She's beautiful, just like her mother, nothing like me.' It was a poignant end to a wonderful interview and I had no idea at the time just how tempestuous the relationship between father and daughter was. Even so, I could tell there was a lot of pride as well as sadness in his voice when he spoke about her.

In 2002 Angelina Jolie made a statement about their relationship: 'My father and I don't speak. I don't hold any anger toward him. I don't believe that somebody's family becomes their blood, because my son's adopted, and families are earned.'

I found him to be a very gentle, handsome man, taller but more frail than I had expected. All I could think of as we spoke was the heartbreaking scene at the end of *The Champ* when he is dying. I couldn't imagine how someone so good-natured

could be so despised by his own daughter that she would file to legally change her surname. Happily, the pair were reunited in early 2010, when Voight joined his daughter, husband Brad Pitt and their children for a holiday in Venice.

A few years before that, when I met Angelina Jolie at the *Alexander the Great* premiere in Dublin, I told her how her father had spoken so enthusiastically about her when I met him and how proud he had sounded. She seemed quite taken aback, because at that time their relationship was at an all-time low. I also told her that when I'd asked for a photo with him, he'd invited me to sit on his knee. She laughed and said, 'Now that's more like it! Did you?'

'Of course I did. He's The Champ, for God's sake!'

She smiled and said, 'I guess he is.'

Kid Rocks!

Two of my favourite interviewees of all time were Kid Rock and P. Diddy, probably because they were both perceived to be the bad boys of rock and hip hop, yet I found them to be anything but.

Kid Rock was over to play his first headline gig in Ireland at the Olympia in Dublin, having supported Bon Jovi at Punchestown earlier that same year. It was a sell-out so there was no real need for him to do any media, but I pushed and pushed. His break-up with Pamela Anderson and subsequent bust-up with her other ex, Tommy Lee, was big news in the world of entertainment. Anderson and Rock had had an 'on again, off again' relationship from 2001 until they married in 2006. They divorced four months later and neither party had spoken about it, or to each other, since then. I wanted the story for the show.

The promoters and his management agreed on a 10-minute interview before the show as long as there was absolutely no mention of Pammy. Of course I agreed, thinking, 'We'll cross that bridge when we come to it!'

When we got to it, though, backstage at the Olympia, it was all very fraught. For starters, there was a reluctance to let myself and my camerawoman, Naomi, into the venue, let alone his dressing room. I suspect that his management had most likely forgotten about the interview, so I made sure to labour the point about how grateful we were to be given access to one of the most successful music artists in the US, how he had a huge following in Ireland and how important the Irish-American connection is, not to mention national TV exposure.

We were finally brought to his dressing room, where it was confirmed that he definitely was not expecting us, as I walked in on him having a hissy fit over teabags. That's right – Kid Rock wanted to make himself a cup of tea and couldn't seem to find the kind he wanted. I took the opportunity to diffuse the situation and break the ice by offering to make him one.

'Who are you?' he asked, noticing for the first time that I was in the room.

'I'm Lorraine, but my family call me Mrs Doyle, because I make the best tea and sandwiches in the country.'

'Who is Mrs Doyle?'

'She's a famous comedy character in a very popular Irish TV show about Catholic priests living on an island.'

'And what are you doing here, besides making tea?'

'I'm also the presenter of Ireland's only entertainment show on TV, pleased to meet you.'

He laughed, probably thinking I was either mentally unstable or that he was being set up as I went about making him a cuppa ('Barry's finest, it's from Cork'). By the time Naomi set up, he had mellowed considerably and actually seemed to be enjoying the conversation.

I steered clear of any potentially volatile subjects until I was sure that he wasn't going to react angrily.

'So I know you said you don't want to talk about Pamela, and I won't ask you what happened, but I'm just wondering how are things between the two of you now?'

> *He definitely was not expecting us, as I walked in on him having a hissy fit over teabags.*

He shot me a look of surprise, suspicion, and then, a smile. 'Well then, if you know I don't want to talk about it, don't ask!'

'But are things OK?'

He laughed. 'I don't see her. I don't know.'

'Are you friends?'

'Not really.'

'Aw, that's sad. Are you upset about that?'

He laughed again. 'Not anymore.'

'Do you talk?'

'If I saw her I'd say hi, but I try to avoid seeing her.'

'Why?'

'I touched the stove, stove was hot. I think, I not touch stove anymore.'

He then told me I was very cheeky, to which I had to agree. I thanked him for his time, his honesty and his resolve. He thanked me for the tea and told me he'd try and find a DVD of Mrs Doyle to remind him of me, which, if I'm honest, isn't exactly how I'd like to be remembered.

A couple of months later, I saw him on *The Ellen DeGeneres Show*. She was also cheeky and apologised in advance of asking him about Pamela Anderson.

It was hilarious to hear him give her the exact same answer about the 'hot stove', but I was happy Ellen, second only to Oprah as queen of chat show hosts in America, hadn't gotten any more out of him than I had.

Queen Elizabeth

I've met and interviewed Liz Hurley on a number of occasions, but it was only during our most recent meeting that I felt like I got to know a little more about 'the real Elizabeth'. It was at brunch, a small gathering of around a dozen ladies organised by mutual friends Aisling Gleeson and Nicola Formby (wife of AA Gill) to celebrate the opening of Liz's new shop at the Kildare Outlet Village.

The food was prepared by the toast of London, our own Michelin star celebrity chef Richard Corrigan, and it was also the first time I was without my cameraman, which not only meant I could relax and enjoy the afternoon, but those around me could too.

We first met almost a decade ago. I was one of a horde of media and public who had gathered at Brown Thomas in Dublin, where she'd been invited to open a new cosmetics hall. I remember thinking how beautiful she was, but in a very natural, real way. She's not a flawless beauty like Christy Turlington or a striking presence like Erin O'Connor, but is attractive in a 'girl next door' kind of way. She has an aspirational but almost-attainable quality about her, which immediately makes her more appealing to women.

Despite all of the mayhem, the distractions of photographers, a meet and greet with fans, an autograph signing and interviews with the waiting press and TV cameras, when I finally got my one-on-one chat with Liz, I remember thinking she was extremely relaxed. She seemed to adore the attention and fuss and was happy to oblige even the oddest of requests (one Irish male in his mid-forties asked her to sign his less than toned beer belly – she giggled and without giving it a second thought scribbled her name as the rest of us laughed with embarrassment for him and admiration for her).

A couple years later, I bumped into her in my favourite Indian restaurant in London (The Star of India on the Old Brompton Road). I said hello, made a note of what she was eating (it's a girl thing – I was curious – and for the record she had a chicken curry, pilau rice and naan bread) and tried to be cool enough not to stare, or at least get caught.

Then in 2006 she came back to Dublin and BT to launch Breast Cancer Awareness Month and we chatted some more. Once again, I asked her the secret of her youthful looks. I reminded her

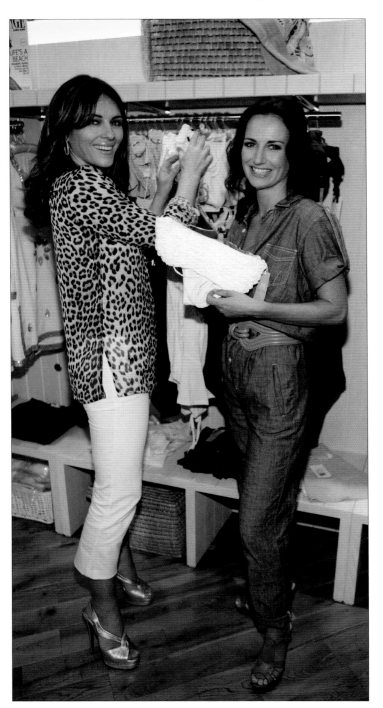

of our meeting in the curry house and she admitted that her days of Indian curries are now few and far between.

'After you reach 40, your metabolism changes. I eat very healthily now,' she said, and admitted that when it comes to preparing for a photo shoot she gets serious and goes on a strict 'nothing but watercress soup' diet for four days. She even said she regularly goes to bed hungry. I have to say that ridiculous as all this is, I really admire her honesty and the fact that she's willing to share her struggle to stay thin with other women who obviously envy her figure.

But then, I would imagine Elizabeth Hurley is a woman's woman, probably influenced by the fact that even as one of the world's most beautiful females, her relationship path hasn't always been a smooth one. Hugh Grant had a much-publicised liaison with a Hollywood prostitute during their twelve years together, then the father of her son Damian (Steve Bing) denied paternity until Elizabeth proved him wrong with a DNA test, but then refused any financial support from the multi-millionaire.

By the time we had brunch together at our last meeting, Elizabeth had married Indian textile heir Arun Nayar and had established herself as a serious businesswoman. She has developed the idea of healthy eating into her own range of guilt-free snacks (which of course you'd have to live on to fit into one of her own range of teeny weeny bikinis) and is proving that she really has got the brains to go with the beauty.

Our dining experience was very informal. We chatted in between eating scrambled eggs and salmon, fish and rice cakes, cold meats and pastries (yes, she got stuck in too) and we even sipped a little pink champagne. She admitted that now she is happily nine pounds heavier than in her thirties – 'You have to be a little heavier in your forties to keep the face looking good' – and that she had tried Botox but didn't like it, as 'I lost my expressions'.

Liz was warm, funny and engaging, despite her slightly off-putting posher-than-posh accent. In fact, her marbles-in-the-mouth manner of speaking belies the down-to-earth party girl within. She mixed and mingled happily with her guests and seemed genuinely delighted to be hosting us.

After brunch, we went shopping. Secretly fancying myself as a Liz Hurley lookalike, I couldn't help myself buying a leopard print bikini *and* full-length kaftan. On my return home, I tried the whole ensemble on for Peter. Unfortunately, he informed me I was more Bet Lynch from *Coronation Street* than Liz. Not exactly the look I was going for!

> *I really admire her honesty and the fact that she's willing to share her struggle to stay thin with other women who obviously envy her figure.*

Mr Nicole Kidman (aka Keith Urban)

I got a call from EMI Records offering me the chance to meet and interview Keith Urban. 'Keith who?' probably wasn't the answer they were expecting, but I had to admit I'd never heard of him before.

'He's Australian, a new country singer, has won Grammy awards, had 10 number one singles in the US charts and has several multiplatinum albums worldwide.'

'Sorry, doesn't ring any bells, but he sounds interesting. When and where?'

The interview was arranged for the Westbury Hotel in Dublin, and when I arrived I began to regret agreeing to it so readily. I was met by an entourage that Mariah Carey would have been proud of: managers, assistants, PAs, stylists, record company reps and music publishers, all with clipboards and demands, all intent on being busy and important.

They wanted a list of the questions I planned to ask (I never read from a list of questions – I do the research, make my notes, memorise them and hope it all stays in my head), they wanted a copy of the interview on DVD before it went to air and they insisted on staying in the room during the interview (yes, all of them). I agreed to all their requests except the DVD before transmission. I didn't have time and *no one* got to pre-approve material before it was broadcast. So after I scribbled down a list of random questions and handed it over, me, Keith Urban and at least a dozen of his closest sidekicks got to meet, greet and speak in the intimate setting of the hotel boardroom.

When he arrived, I quickly realised that it was a case of the people surrounding the star having bigger egos than the star himself. He greeted me warmly and was extremely amiable for the entire interview.

He spoke about his drug and alcohol addictions and how he became a frequent user of cocaine when he first went to Nashville. In 1998, having hit rock bottom, he checked into a treatment centre, cleaned up his act and then released his self-titled American debut album. Success after success followed in America and Australia and his plan was to emulate that across Europe.

It was later, off camera and when the entourage had begun to lose interest, that he let his guard down a bit and talked about being on the road and how that affected his relationships, and how difficult it was to keep them together. I knew that he had dated a veterinarian for eight years, then proposed, but split a year later. He was then rumoured to be dating American supermodel Niki Taylor. I asked him if was seeing anyone at the moment. After a little coaxing he did say that he had just recently started dating someone very high profile who was also in the entertainment business and was also from Australia. He told me it was still very early in their relationship, so they hadn't gone public, but that he was very excited and had no doubt I'd hear about it very soon. Sure enough, a few months after our meeting it was announced that he and Nicole Kidman were a couple. After a year together they married and now have a daughter, Sunday Rose Kidman Urban.

I've met Nicole twice and she definitely doesn't wear her heart on her sleeve. On both occasions I couldn't help wondering why on earth she even goes through with the promotional and touring schedule. She was quite obviously uncomfortable, didn't smile once, gave very curt replies to all questions and when I asked her if everything was OK she replied, 'I don't like interviews.'

In my opinion, marrying someone like Keith Urban, who is grounded and personable, is the best thing that could have happened to her. After splitting from Tom Cruise, she apparently dated Liz Hurley's ex, Steve Bing (or 'Bing Laden', as the British tabloids labelled him after the way he treated Liz), then got engaged to womanising rocker Lenny Kravitz. Talk about 'out of the frying pan'!

The marriage has resulted in a whole new level of media scrutiny for Urban. It was reported that he was involved in a crash on his way from an AA meeting to his home in Sydney. A paparazzi photographer was chasing him and caused him to skid off his motorbike, resulting in injury and damage. The photographer helped him and didn't take any photos at the scene. Urban later released a statement through his publicist saying the incident was 'the result of one person's desire to do his job and my desire to maintain my privacy'. This sums up the character of the man – no legal proceedings, no retaliation, no drama. Nicole is one lucky lady and I sincerely hope this love lasts.

When he arrived, I quickly realised that it was a case of the people surrounding the star having bigger egos than the star himself.

Will Smith

Flattery will get you everywhere, but when you're talking about my shoes, Will, flattery gets you publicity for your new film. My lasting impression of Will Smith is that he admired my shoes, a fact that would go unnoticed by most, but for a serious, self-confessed shoe addict like myself, it's not only a moment worth remembering, it's worth celebrating and documenting.

I find Will Smith to be incredibly handsome, and on the day we met he was also friendly and entertaining, which is particularly impressive considering I was number 12 on his list of 30 interviews he had to get through.

The said pair of shoes also just so happened to be one of my favourites, a pair of blue suede Eileen Shields pumps. When I told him as much and that the designer was Irish and had just moved permanently to New York, he became almost as excited as me. We chatted mostly about the shoes, our mothers (a devoted son, he calls her every day) and, of course, the movie. Before I left, I gave him Eileen's details as he stated, 'I really need to get a pair for Jada, she would *love* those.'

It was years later when I finally got to meet Eileen Shields at the Irish Tatler Women of the Year Awards. We were both being honoured – I accepted the entertainment award and Eileen was recognised for the international success of her label. At this stage she had a long list of celebrity clients, including the girls from *Sex and the City* and *Desperate Housewives* (she designed a pair of shoes for Eva Longoria, aptly named the Eva, which she wore in every colour on the show) and Jada Pinkett Smith.

'I told her about you,' I said. 'Well, actually, I told her husband about you.'

'Wow, really? Thank you.'

Jimmy Choo designed shoes for Princess Diana, Beyoncé wrote and performed a song simply entitled, and dedicated to, 'Louboutins' and Manolo Blahnik named a pair the SJP (after Sarah Jessica Parker). Surely my little bit of Hollywood networking entitles me to the ultimate accolade for a shoe addict – a pair of shoes named in my honour? I'm not sure 'the Lorraines' would have quite the same ring to it, though I live in hope!

P. Diddy – Bad Boy of Hip Hop?

P. Diddy, Puff Daddy, Sean Combs – I'm not sure what he was calling himself at the time I met him, but I had read all the stories about how the head of Bad Boy Records had been charged with possession of firearms, aggravated assault, intimidation and bribery. His friend The Notorious B.I.G. was shot dead after an awards ceremony in LA, one of his recording sessions was interrupted by gunfire and on a night out with then girlfriend Jennifer Lopez he had to flee the scene of a gun battle in a New York nightclub. This was going to be no regular interview.

And he was having woman trouble! He had just broken up with Lopez (all those gunfights and court cases must wreak havoc on romance) after two very 'eventful' years, and she married one of her back-up dancers, Chris Judd, a few months later. Sean (he said I could call him Sean) felt it necessary to address the situation by releasing a statement to the American press saying that he hadn't been faithful to

J-Lo, but had enjoyed rekindling his relationship with his ex (and father of his son), Kimberly Porter.

As expected, there was a 'nothing personal' clause in my interview with the rapper, and this time I told my superiors I would be sticking to it. I had no intentions of annoying someone who allegedly employs members of the Crips LA gang to provide his security. Basically, I was nervous. He was late. I waited. I waited two hours, in fact, and the longer I waited, the more nervous I became.

Finally I was told by his 'heavies' (never before has a title been so appropriate), 'Mr Combs is on his way. Please take a seat.' From behind the stage appeared a man of average height and stature (possibly around 5'9" and slim build), walking towards me with hand already outstretched and smiling. He was not what I had expected. He was apologetic, attentive and charming, and when I asked him what I should call him, he replied, 'You can call me Sean, for all my Irish brothers out there.'

We spoke about his records, the tour and his business ventures outside the record label. He has a clothing line, a men's aftershave, a restaurant chain and his own brand of vodka. With an estimated worth of $350 million, it's no wonder this bad boy from the housing projects in Harlem has a few enemies, but his charm and charisma won me over.

'You can come hang with me anytime,' he offered as we were given the cue to wrap it up. I thanked him and said I just might take him up on that some day. As we left, I couldn't help thinking to myself, 'Now what could I possibly wear that would go with a flak jacket?'

Onstage with 'Diddy' in Dublin

You can call me Sean, for all my Irish brothers out there.

Did I disappoint YOU?

(well, yes, actually...)

O f all the interviews I've done over all the years, very few have been unpleasant experiences. Even those few interviewees who started out frosty usually warmed up by the time we said goodbye. I could put this down to one of two things: my wonderful ability to defrost even the coldest of characters with my endearing charm and personality, or the fact that there was a camera in their face and therefore they would be rather foolish to show anything but their best side for the short time they had to endure me. Let's be honest – it was the latter. Some, however, didn't care either way. So this chapter is for the egomaniacs who made my job difficult and for those who 'turned it on' as soon as the camera turned over. Roll the outtakes...

Barry McCall has taken some of my favourite photos over the years. This is one of them, for the Irish Tatler November 2009 cover, wearing Annoushka jewellery and a FCUK French Connection dress.

Hurt's So Good

Never meet your heroes? In my experience I'd say that's nonsense, as they rarely disappoint. However, meeting John Hurt was an exception to the rule (OK, there are a few exceptions, but we'll get to those later).

There aren't many living legends in the entertainment world, but John Hurt is surely one. As the voice of Hazel in *Watership Down* to the crazy, incarcerated Max in *Midnight Express*, John Merrick in *The Elephant Man* and 'The Bird' O'Donnell in *The Field*, all are unique, compelling performances from a real acting talent.

It was the day before the premiere of *Night Train*, which he starred in with Brenda Blethyn. I was entertainment correspondent with TV3 at the time and had requested an interview with John and Brenda. Unfortunately the actors weren't available for sit-down interviews, so my only chance was to try to get a word from either or both of them at the premiere. It also meant it wasn't compulsory for me to see the movie beforehand, which meant I was under less pressure, but I was disappointed. I rarely even had time to sit down and eat lunch, never mind take time out to watch a movie. However, on the night, John and Brenda changed their minds and said that after the red carpet they would give me a one-on-one interview. I would miss dinner again, but hey, I got the interview – result! I was delighted.

> *You obviously don't want to be here, John, so why don't we just forget this.*

First up was Brenda Blethyn. She was charming, endearing and funny – all I wanted her to be. John Hurt, on the other hand, was less than happy to be there, which he made very clear with his short, sharp, monosyllabic answers. He was decidedly uncommunicative, so much so that I did something I've never done in an interview situation – I told him.

I said, 'You obviously don't want to be here, John, so why don't we just forget this. The only reason I'm here is because I have always admired you as an actor – I'm actually working overtime at the moment, for which I don't get paid, to give you the opportunity to plug your movie. But if you don't appreciate that, let's just leave it.'

I stood up and made for the door. To my shock and relief, John also stood up and apologised and implored me to stay. Reluctantly, I did, and we continued with the interview. He was very pleasant after that and I have to say that I respected him more after the experience. He wasn't afraid to apologise and I will always admire him for that. He was obviously just having an off day – even celebrities have those.

Storm in a Teacup

Even though I've never been a fan, I still appreciate that there must be something appealing about Daniel O'Donnell (although I still can't understand it). Hundreds of thousands of fans around the globe can't be that wrong, and he's sold over 10 million records. So as always, I did my research and set up my first-ever meeting with the inspiration for *Father Ted*'s Eoin McLove character with an open mind.

My father is the founder member of Ireland's longest-running and most successful show band, The Indians, and I thought that this fact would be appreciated by Daniel. We would have an immediate rapport. We knew the show band scene, we grew up around the business, we had something in common. With this little ace up my sleeve, I was quietly confident that this interview could be his most revealing yet.

I hadn't thought I would have to play my trump card so soon. For a full 10 minutes before the cameras started rolling I did all I could, ace and all, to try to establish an affinity with wee Daniel, so much so that my cameraman, Owen, got a fit of the giggles. I tried everything. I complimented him, I told him stories about my dad's band, I even tried telling a joke, but he blanked me. Nothing. I couldn't believe that the Monarch of the Mammies Tea Party was turning out to be the most aloof person I had ever met.

Then Owen shouted, 'We're rolling,' and the red light came on. I will never forget what happened next. Daniel – cold, aloof, unfriendly Daniel – leaned over, put his hand on my lap and said with a well-worn smile and that showbiz twinkle in his eye, 'I have to start off by saying it's such a pleasure to meet you, Lorraine.'

I nearly got sick. I wanted to push his hand off my lap and say, 'What? You just blanked me for the last 10 minutes, until you knew the camera was switched on. You are a fake, Daniel O'Donnell, with your insipid warbling and your "I'll make you a cup of tea" sweeter than sweet persona. I bet you haven't made a cup of tea in your life for fear of staining one of your lemon Pringle sweaters!' But I couldn't. I had to bite my lip – until now.

Something's Got Me Started

> *Let's just say he became 'Simply Redder' as he fumed his way through the interview.*

I have to confess that I liked Simply Red. I use the past tense because meeting Mick Hucknall has made it very difficult to enjoy his music since then. He takes the term 'self-confident' to a whole new level. Put it this way – if he was chocolate, he'd eat himself. You would think that having ditched his band and experienced a slump in sales as a solo artist, his attitude would be different. Unfortunately not! I'm not denying the man is talented; it's just a shame that someone so successful and privileged fails to recognise the important role media exposure has played in his career achievements to date.

Mick arrived an hour late. No problem there – celebrities are rarely on time and as long as my deadline isn't for that very day it isn't a problem. That particular day I had done an earlier interview with Sophie Dahl that had been sent back to base for transmission that evening, so we were under no pressure. But when he eventually arrived, there was no apology from Mick. He strutted his way into the Four Seasons hotel room we had booked for the rendezvous and sat down with jacket and shades still on, declaring, 'Can we make this quick? I don't have much time.'

'Of course,' I said. 'We're all set up and ready to go. I'm Lorraine, by the way, and a big fan. We've met before.' I got a wet fish handshake. I was surprised, as the first time I met Mick he had been over-attentive in a touchy-feely kind of way. This time, he was just touchy, as in irritable.

My cameraman politely suggested that Mr Hucknall might like to take his sunglasses off because he was getting a bad reflection off the glass. At this point I have to note that it was a policy in TV3 to kindly suggest to all interviewees that they remove their shades where at all possible, as it comes across as being impersonal and is off-putting for the viewer. Even Bono had obliged on plenty of occasions.

Oops! Mick didn't like that. He launched into a tirade: 'Who do you think you are, telling me what to wear? I will wear what I want.'

He was being so dismissive, especially to my cameraman, that I decided to go a step further and stir it up. I suggested he take off his leather coat too as it actually made him look chunky – unless, of course, he was happy to look 'bulkier than normal'. I knew (as was my intention) that I had hit a nerve with that one. Let's just say he became 'Simply Redder' as he fumed his way through the interview.

I can't say it was my best work (actually, it was terrible), but I did get some satisfaction from the fact he was even less comfortable than I was about the whole meeting. What I did get from the interview is that he showed himself in a true light – to be anything but the soft-centred, broken-hearted crooner I had been a fan of.

'If you don't know me by now'? Oh yes I do, and I will never, never, never want to know you again!

My first meeting with Mick Hucknall, pictured here, was a more pleasant one

Saving Silent Ryan

I went into the Meg Ryan interview wide-eyed, perhaps even star-struck, not quite ignorant but a little innocent and completely unprepared for what was to come.

For years afterwards I worried about what went wrong and questioned the way I had handled it. Maybe it was my fault. Had I inadvertently offended her?

When people ask me what she was like and I tell them honestly that she was one of the most uncooperative and dismissive people I have ever had the misfortune to meet, they can't and won't believe me. No way, not sweet, twinkle in her eye, rom-com queen *You've Got Mail* Meg? Surely not! But then the infamous Michael Parkinson interview happened and I was vindicated (more on that later).

I was quite new to the job and was still wildly enthusiastic about getting up in the middle of the night to get to the airport in time for the first plane to London. I had a folder full of notes and spent the journey going over my research not only on Meg, but her then husband, Dennis Quaid (who, incidentally, nearly made this chapter too). What a bonus for TV3 – two A-listers in one day, and all on the film company's PR expense account.

I arrived at the hotel and was brought to the suite to meet Meg. I said hello but got no response. I smiled, but still nothing. I started dishing out the compliments, which were sincere and heartfelt: 'I'm a huge fan', 'I love the new movie' (*You've Got Mail*), etc., etc. I even tried the when all else fails, girl bonding fail-safe line – 'Where did you get those shoes?' – but no dice. *When Lorraine Met Sally* was rapidly turning into *Speechless in Seattle*.

I informed her that my next port of call, so to speak, was her husband, as he was also on the promo tour circuit. As they had worked onset together before and were now obviously touring together, I suggested it must be wonderful to be able to combine two working trips. She scowled and said, 'I have made it clear that I am not here to discuss anything personal.' I apologised and explained I wasn't prying, just pointing out that it must be nice not having to spend that time apart.

'Do I have to continue with this?' she bellowed.

'No,' I replied, 'not at all. If you'll excuse me, I have another interview to get to.'

My relief at having escaped that torture was tempered by a feeling of shock and huge disappointment. When something similarly excruciating, but which lasted

When Lorraine Met Sally was rapidly turning into Speechless in Seattle.

Tinseltown and Lorraine

For nine years I had been trying to convince TV3 that they should be represented at the Oscars. Budgets were always the issue, despite the fact that for the cost of a couple of flights and a cheap hotel room they would have had the most inexpensive 'one-off special' TV show in their programming schedule.

In 2008, *Xposé* was almost a year old and we were still working hard at establishing the brand and always looking at ways of improving the show. I was so determined that *Xposé* would be at the Oscars in our first year that I had to resort to the most unethical of journalistic practices, something we do when all else fails – I lied through my teeth.

Publisher PJ Gibbons (*Social & Personal* magazine) had told me that the interior designer of the green room at the Oscars (the holding area backstage for presenters, performers and nominees) was Irish, so I tracked him down and phoned him late one night from home. I quickly learned that he was only a fraction Irish ('I think my great-grandfather came from County Killarney'), but if it's good enough for the Irish football team, then it's good enough for me. I sweet talked my long-lost Irish cousin into allowing me and my camera access to the green room on the day of the ceremony. Not actually *during* the ceremony, you understand, just earlier in the day, when there would be no one around.

My sales pitch to the station was a work of fiction worthy of a nomination itself. I boasted about access to the best parties. I explained that I had lots of interviews lined up. I named fictitious contacts with convincing surnames ending in '–stein' and '–berg'. And of course I told them that my new best friend, who happens to be Irish, is getting me into the green room! And then there was the *green* carpet – the US-Ireland Alliance was hosting their third annual Oscar Wilde: Honoring the Irish in Film pre-Academy Awards party (or the 'Irish Oscars') the night before at the Wilshire Ebell in LA. That year they were honouring James L. Brooks, Fiona Shaw and Colm Meaney, and Jack Nicholson was going to be presenting the awards. Jack Nicholson? You can't get more A-list than that.

We could go (me, a cameraman and assistant producer) on the basis that we hired a car, drove ourselves around and stayed in a hotel off the main drag. Like a teenage girl who'd just been told by her parents that she could go to the kids' disco as long as she was home by 11 and didn't wear a mini-skirt, I was elated. Yes, there were a few conditions, but I didn't care – I was going to Hollywood! I was on my way to the Oscars!

> *I sweet talked my long-lost Irish cousin into allowing me and my camera access to the green room on the day of the ceremony.*

With or without an invitation to the Oscars, I was red carpet-ready in this Delphine Grandjouan creation

Myself and Glen Hansard go back a long way (this was taken prior to their gig in the RDS), so to meet up with him on the day he won an Oscar was particularly special

I had been given approval only three days before departure and four days before the event. That same night, I got a call from Mr Interior O'Designer to say he was sorry, but the Kodak Theatre green room was a no-go area the day of the show, and could we do it tomorrow? Of course we couldn't, as we weren't arriving in LA until the evening before showtime, but I kept this minor setback to myself.

The next morning I was called into the office by the powers that be. They had been thinking about this whole Oscars thing and were beginning to really warm to the idea, so much so that now they wanted not one, but two *Xposé* shows from there, as well as a one-hour Oscars special show and two live link broadcasts to the *Ireland AM* breakfast show. A sponsor had come on board for the one-hour special, which made the sales and finance departments very happy.

'Does this mean we can upgrade to a nicer hotel?' I asked, trying to salvage something from a very ominous situation.

'No.'

'What about getting a driver?'

'No, get a sat nav.'

> *Suddenly, the teenage disco queen had just been told she'd have to bring her younger brother and his ugly friends.*

Suddenly, the teenage disco queen had just been told she'd have to bring her younger brother and his ugly friends. I had nothing set up, no contacts, no experience of the event and no accreditation, and now I had a sponsor to please and a one-hour TV special to fill.

Even if I was able to fight my way through security to get near the red carpet (which was highly unlikely), I would be at the back of a four-deep line of heavyweight international broadcasters vying for a glimpse, never mind an interview. On any red carpet, your position is based on three things: territory, network and ratings. Ireland is one of the smallest territories because we only broadcast on our island (to a population the size of Phoenix, Arizona), so no points for that one! TV3 isn't the state broadcaster and is small in comparison to other networks, even within Europe – still nil points. And *Xposé*, although doing well, had a comparatively insignificant audience. In the ratings game, the bigger the audience, the better the view, which meant no place on the red carpet for us.

I left the meeting with a smile on my face, but inside I was having a panic attack.

I sat at my desk frantically phoning, texting and emailing anyone I could think of who might have a Hollywood connection.

Glen Hansard and Marketa Irglova were nominated in the Best Original Song category. I've interviewed Glen many times and plugged tours for his band, The Frames, over the years. Surely he would be able to meet up and do an interview? I left messages but got no replies.

Saoirse Ronan was nominated in that year's Best Supporting Actress category. Again, after calls to Saoirse, her mum, dad, agent and even her aunt, I got nothing back. I made numerous other attempts to speak to, meet up with and get numbers from many other actors, managers and even journalists, but it just wasn't happening. This is usually where Plan B would come into effect, but I didn't have one.

That night, lying awake and thinking of the mess I was in, I realised I didn't have an American visa. My first reaction was, 'Thank God! This could be my saving grace and way out.' But the next day when I made enquiries, the American embassy pulled out all the stops and had my passport stamped and ready that evening.

The first time something actually went right with this trip was on the flight to LA. As we boarded the Aer Lingus plane, a friendly air steward (yes, those kind of airlines do still exist) steered us left and we were upgraded to business class. Knowing that from the moment we touched down in LAX the rest of our trip would be 'cattle class', we were most appreciative. We all enjoyed the in-flight service, while I read through my notes and began drafting lines for links. I had resigned myself to the fact that all parts of the shows I was doing might just have to involve me talking to a camera in front of famous Hollywood landmarks.

We had experienced a particularly miserable February and March weather-wise in Ireland that year, so we were really looking forward to some California sunshine. As we disembarked, we could hear the rain pelting off the exit tunnel. It took us almost three hours to get our luggage, pass through security, find the rental car and leave the airport. We didn't have enough time to check into the hotel and change, as we were already late for the Oscar Wilde party, somewhere I thought I might be able to 'network' and make some contacts that would result in interviews. It was also renowned as one of the best parties during Oscar week. Not exactly dressed for the

> *In the ratings game, the bigger the audience, the better the view, which meant no place on the red carpet for us.*

We could have hung out with Seamus all day. Originally we had asked for just 10 minutes of his time, but one hour (and one very tired and sore cameraman) later, we stopped talking. It was an interviewer's dream, but an editor's nightmare. Between that and the other two interviews, as well as intros to all the pieces, we had a long night of editing ahead.

Never let a story get in the way of good shopping!

Our last day in Los Angeles was spent filming general shots, promos (to promote the Oscar special that was now being called 'Gate-crashing the Governors Ball') and programme links and intros. It was our first sunny day since we arrived, so we headed to Sunset Boulevard, and of course it was glorious. I remember being surrounded by the most exquisite shops but had no time to explore them. Then I came up with the genius idea of filming the links with me walking in and out of shops. The guys couldn't understand why it took me nine attempts to get the take for one link where I was coming out of the Guess shop. When we finally had the right one, I nipped back in, paid for my purchases and arrived out laden down with bags like a true pro. Never let a story get in the way of good shopping!

Those precious master tapes made it all the way from Sunset Boulevard to Ballymount Industrial Estate. The shows aired, the ratings were good and the sponsors were happy. It was by far the hardest week's work I have ever done, and I've slogged through a muddy music festival over three days while eight months pregnant. Would I do it all over again?

Are you California dreamin'?

The Ones Who Made Me Laugh

Interviewing comedians can sometimes be challenging and always unpredictable, but never boring. Much like working with children and animals, I always approach these interviews with caution. They have provided some great TV moments – even when the joke was on me – but I realise that it wasn't always the funny guys who made me laugh…

Mock the Week? He Makes My Week

'You wouldn't happen to be going anywhere near Rathmines, would you?'

The 2002 annual Barretstown Gala Ball had just ended, and as we left we met Dara Ó'Briain standing outside, looking for a lift home. This would have been less surprising had he not just worked all night as MC and auctioneer (raising over €200,000), but Dara isn't one for diva demands. When he had finished a long night's work, he left quietly to make his own way home, with the gift of a bottle of white wine under his arm – 'I have a lot of catching up to do.'

All we could offer him was the space in the boot of our friend's jeep, as there were already a few couples doubling up on their partners' laps in the back. Dara gladly accepted. 'I've travelled home from gigs in worse, and anyway, I don't think the night bus extends to the Wicklow Mountains.'

You would think that having spent over five hours onstage that evening he'd be all talked out, but Dara kept us laughing all the way home. He hadn't eaten all night and asked to be dropped at a takeaway near his place in Rathmines. The only place open at 2 a.m. was Abrakebabra. 'I know the chef,' he said. 'I'll ask him to recommend something to complement this cheeky little Sauvignon Blanc.'

Later that year I was in Edinburgh covering the Fringe Festival. I was due to finish work on Friday and fly home, but I opted to stay for the weekend, see some friends and enjoy Dara's new stand-up show. His turned out to be the hottest ticket of the festival, selling out every night. One reviewer wrote, 'If you don't laugh at Ó'Briain, check your pulse, you must be dead.' After the show, we met up for a few drinks and he took it upon himself to show myself and Peter around his new 'home away from home'.

He was genuinely excited about the buzz he was creating, not just at the festival, but among his ever-increasing UK audience. As we moved from pub to pub, we spoke about everything from incorporating theoretical physics into his show (he studied it in University College Dublin) to the subtleties of traditionally pressed scrumpy cider. We compared not-so-shaggy dog stories about racing greyhounds (we were both owners) and debated why pre-marriage courses should include either a *Never Mind the Buzzcocks* or *Question of Sport*-type quiz which the bride-to-be had to study for.

I was amazed at how enthusiastic, fresh and up-to-the-minute his earlier performance was, considering he was near the end of a month-long run. He explained that he tries to change each show slightly by including something that's very current in the news or relevant to the festival or locals. One particular gag at the start of the show I saw was a perfect example of this.

Dara Ó'Briain has been described as 'Terry Wogan's heir apparent as Britain's favourite Irishman'.

We were still trying to come to terms with the fact that Ireland had been cruelly knocked out of the 2002 World Cup by Spain. The Irish, complete underdogs, had played brilliantly and ended the match level at 1-1 before the dramatic, heartbreaking penalty shoot-out. Dara's opening line was, 'I'm Dara Ó'Briain, Irish comedian. Basically this means that for 89 minutes I'm going to be fantastic and make you cry laughing, but then in the last minute, some little Spanish f**ker is going to jump up onstage, tell the best gag of the night and steal the show!'

By the time we had to leave the last bar in a city of many late-night license extensions, I couldn't help feeling that maybe I was partly responsible for what might end up being a somewhat subdued performance the following night. 'Not at all,' was the reply. 'Sure, I don't start work till 9 o'clock at night.'

A couple of years later, his show at Edinburgh ended up being the biggest-selling solo comedy show of the festival. He then went on to present the highly successful panel show *Mock the Week* on BBC2 and was co-presenter of *Three Men in a Boat*, along with Griff Rhys Jones and Rory McGrath, also for the BBC.

It's no wonder Dara Ó'Briain has been described as 'Terry Wogan's heir apparent as Britain's favourite Irishman'. He is as charming, intelligent and incredibly funny offstage as he is on. I will gladly go out of my way to give him a lift home anytime!

That Lorraine
K Thing

Peter Kay and wife Susan arrive at the Four Seasons Hotel, Dublin, for Keith Duffy's party

B y way of an apology to the fabulous Peter Kay, I will relate this story, against myself, for your amusement and hope that he forgives me.

In a moment of madness, tiredness and hormonal imbalance (I was seven months pregnant), I embarrassed myself and, more importantly, Peter Kay at an event he was attending in aid of charity.

We all know how much work Keith Duffy does for Irish Autism Action, and I help him out whenever I can. Most of the time, this involves joining him to co-host or act as MC for a fundraising event. One of the many annual events he organises is a celebrity golf classic in Dublin and it's always well attended by his show business pals from the UK and Ireland. One particular year, more than a dozen cast members from *Coronation Street* made the trip over, as well as Peter Kay and his wife. I was more than happy to cover the event for *Entertainment News* and also for the paper I was writing for at the time. When I arrived at the prearranged photo call I was surrounded by the *Corrie* girls (who had travelled for the party that night, not the golf) and was bombarded with questions about the very obvious bump I was carrying. Of course I recognised them all, being a fan of the soap, and when I had done the interview it was time for a press photo.

All this time, there was a rather large, quiet character hanging in the background who I hadn't really noticed and presumed was the partner of one of the girls. It was suggested that I stand at the front for the picture, with everyone lined up behind me and my bump. The aforementioned character made to join the gang for the picture and I politely asked, 'Sorry, would you mind if I just get one with the girls?'

The girls all cracked up laughing, and he backed away apologetically.

Later, as we left to make our way back to studio, my cameraman practically screamed at me, 'Don't you know who that was?'

'Who are you talking about?'

'The guy you just dissed. That was Peter Kay. You just told Peter Kay to get out of the photo. *Peter Kay!*'

My heart sank. I felt so bad. *Of course* it was Peter Kay, I realised in hindsight. But in my defence, can I just say that I had never seen *That Peter Kay Thing* or *Live at the Top of the Tower*. I had only seen *Phoenix Nights*, in which he plays wheelchair user Brian Potter, owner of the Phoenix Club. In character, as well as being in a wheelchair, his hair colour is different and he wears a moustache and glasses. It's one of my favourite comedy shows, and what's worse, it is a favourite of many of my family members. When I reluctantly told them the story, I received a tirade of abuse

> *'The guy you just dissed. That was Peter Kay. You just told Peter Kay to get out of the photo. Peter Kay!'*

I'll never hear the end of. What makes matters worse is how well Peter Kay handled it. He made himself available at the photo call but wasn't pushy. When asked to step aside, he did so without taking offence. If he hadn't been so bloody nice I wouldn't feel so bad about it.

Seven years later at a family dinner, during a very rare pause in the conversation, my brother-in-law Padraig said something completely out of the blue and totally unrelated to what we had all been talking about previously: 'I still can't believe you did that to Peter Kay.'

Maybe now that I've come clean I'll be forgiven?

The Coronation Street *girls get to grips with my bump!*

Jesus Christ Sleepy Star

It was like a meet and greet with royalty the night Andrew Lloyd Webber came to Dublin for the opening night of *Jesus Christ Superstar*. About 20 journalists-in-waiting were lined up outside the Point Depot when his limo pulled up. There was an air of excitement and anticipation, as this was the first time the show had come to Ireland, and the fact that its creator was also here added to the importance of the event.

The organisers had pulled out all the stops to try to make the venue as glamorous as possible, since back then it was basically a warehouse, but Dublin's North Wall is no West End, and Sir Andrew made his journey amidst a cavalcade of ferry-bound articulated trucks and neighbouring construction site traffic.

As he stepped from the car, I saw him close up and in person for the first time, and all those images of his Spitting Image puppet from the 1980s and 1990s came flooding back. The only way I can describe it is that it was like coming face to face with a cartoon character – like meeting Scooby Doo!

Unfortunately, I had this thought in my mind as he filed along the meet and greet line and I began to giggle. I told my cameraman and he started laughing too. I was next up, and the local PR person who was introducing us shot me a look as if to say, 'Are you serious? Don't let me down!' With a grin as permanent as my own Spitting Image puppet, I said hello and excused myself for giggling, explaining that I was so nervous and excited to meet him that I couldn't contain myself. He seemed quite flattered, and being the gentleman that he is, stopped to chat with me a little longer before moving on. Thank God I pulled it together for the latter part of the interview.

With that over, I had been invited to watch the show, and as it was my first week back at work after maternity leave (and my first night out in ages), I was quite looking forward to it. The hubby, however, wasn't as enthusiastic. Peter is one of those musicians who believes musical theatre is made by people who can't make up their mind whether they want a career in music or acting, and for people who don't like either.

Despite this, he joined me for our night out at what would have normally been our bedtime as new parents. When we got to our seats it looked as though we were in the same row as Sir Andrew, just four seats down from where he was sitting. Surely some mistake?

'No, he thought you were very sweet, and because you were so nervous and are such a big fan, he wanted you to have the best seats in the house,' the PR lady explained.

I acknowledged him, mouthed a 'thank you' as the lights went down and sat back to enjoy the show. The enjoyment was short lived. As I mentioned, Peter and I had recently become parents. Emelia was only four months old, and anyone who's been there will know that a young baby equals sleep deprivation. Ten minutes into the first half, Peter fell asleep. But not in a quiet, eyes closed, nobody-will-notice kind of way. No, it was in a pretty spectacular way, actually, as good as any of the theatrical displays I was witnessing onstage.

His head would fall down, chin hit his chest, a grunt, then a rhythmic nodding of the head while trying to find a comfortable position. Head falls backward, mouth opens and S-N-O-R-E! I gave his leg a little squeeze. He woke up with a rather loud, disoriented mumble: 'What? What? Oh, sorry.' It felt like the entire row was enjoying Peter's performance more than the cast's.

I spent the first half watching Peter, who made at least three more attempts to nod off, and I don't think I have ever been happier to see an interval. We went outside for a bit of fresh air and decided that rather than put both of us through a similar second half, we should just go. I knew I could come back and see the show with one of my sisters or my mum another night, but we couldn't leave two empty seats beside Sir Andrew. With that, Peter spotted an American couple walking down from the upper level towards the merchandise stand. He made up the excuse that we had to get back home immediately, as we had just received a call from the babysitter. We didn't want to insult Mr Lloyd Webber by leaving two empty seats beside him, so would they be so kind as to do us a favour and take our seats for the second half? At first they were suspicious and asked if it was for real as they looked at out ticket stubs. When we eventually persuaded them that they weren't being set up, they were delighted, thanked us and hugged each other as we ran for the exit.

> *Ten minutes into the first half, Peter fell asleep. But not in a quiet, eyes closed, nobody-will-notice kind of way.*

Girls on Top

One of my earliest and favourite TV memories is of my family sitting down to watch *French and Saunders* together in the late 1980s. It was topical, irreverent and incredibly funny and always had wonderful cameo appearances by mostly B-list celebrities, at whose expense we all had a good laugh. Their spoof sketches on movies of the moment (*Misery*, *Thelma and Louise*, *Titanic*, *The Silence of the Lambs* and *Lord of the Rings*) and pop stars (The Corrs, Madonna, Bananarama and Sonia) were hilarious and they developed a cast of characters, played by themselves, that became reference points for modern British culture.

So when I was offered the opportunity to interview them, why was I filled with a sense of total elation yet also complete dread and fear? Of course I wanted to meet my TV heroines – I had grown up with them and felt that I had known them for most

French and Saunders warm up in their dressing room

of my life. But I also knew that in an interview situation, their razor-sharp wit and unpredictability could leave you looking like a complete lemon! I decided to throw caution to the wind and meet up with the dangerous duo, and what do you know, all my suspicions were confirmed.

All started well, and in the pre-interview banter they were both polite and seemed to genuinely take it as a compliment that I had been a fan for so long. After a quick chat about Dublin, shopping, restaurants and other miscellaneous topics, the interview began. By now I felt completely at ease and was relaxed enough to admit to them that initially I'd had a real feeling of trepidation about this interview. Dawn seemed concerned. 'Aw, whatever for, darling? What were you worried about?'

'About what you might do. I've seen some of your interviews before,' I replied with a laugh.

'Were you scared that maybe I might just get up,' at which point she got up, 'and walk over to you,' oh my God, she's coming over, 'and sit right down on top of you and make you do the whole interview like this?'

Dawn French was sitting on top of me. My first reaction was to laugh, after which I could hardly catch my breath, which meant speaking was out of the question. I tried to ask something, but a combination of laughter and breathlessness made it impossible. She more or less conducted the interview for what seemed like an age, with Jennifer contributing occasionally to her monologue.

The camera was rolling for the duration and the producers loved it. They ran the entire piece, which was more of a *French and Saunders* sketch than an interview, but I'm proud to say I was part of it!

It's Not a Drag, It's a Compliment

Oscar Wilde once said that the only thing worse than being talked about is *not* being talked about, which is never more true than when it relates to comedians lampooning TV personalities. The *Après Match* trio of Risteárd Cooper, Barry Murphy and Gary Cooke first began presenting their brilliant comedy shows during Ireland's World Cup qualifying games in 1998. Initially, the theme was football and they regularly made fun of resident RTÉ pundits Bill O'Herlihy, Eamon Dunphy and Johnny Giles, but as their shows grew in popularity, they cast the net a little wider and dragged radio and TV personalities and even politicians into the frame.

I can't remember exactly when it was, but after one of the Ireland matches the 'real' RTÉ coverage ended and the spoof began. It opened with a shot of a news desk, one that looked remarkably like the TV3 news desk, and the newsreader introduced 'Lorraine with the entertainment news'. Barry Murphy appeared with a black wig, false eyelashes, a lot of badly applied lipstick and wearing a black sequin dress. He smiled the most affected, gormless smile, flicked his wig and said nothing. Then there was the sound of a toilet flushing and Martin King (played by Risteárd) appeared from behind the green screen backdrop to present the weather. It was brilliant! I was with a group of friends who didn't know whether to laugh or feign outrage, but when they saw my reaction, they knew I was more complimented than offended. I had made it onto *Après Match*, for God's sake! I was up there with Bill, Eamon, Johnny, Gerry Ryan, George Hamilton, Gary Lineker, George Hook and even Brian Cowen.

Ratings for the show were huge (in the region of 700,000), so for weeks after I was greeted with, 'Saw you on *Après Match*!' The team then developed a few new characters – three Irish fans from Dublin who sat on the couch drinking cans of beer, commenting on everything from the technical dexterity of Liam Brady's left foot to the tenderness of a bison's hoop (just Google it, I couldn't possibly try to elaborate). Behind the green jersey-clad geniuses is a large poster of me on their sitting room wall.

Not long after all the *Après Match* excitement, I was invited to dinner in my friend Norah Casey's house. As we took our seats, Barry Murphy came over, and looking very uncomfortable, noticed that he was seated beside me. I could tell he was trying to gauge my reaction, so I thought I'd wind him up a bit. I pretended to be standoffish.

'So, you're Lorraine in the *Après Match* sketches?'

'Eh, yes.'

'I suppose you think that's funny?'

'Eh, well, yes, actually.'

'Me too, but don't you know that sequins are *so* last year, Barry!'

> " *Barry Murphy appeared with a black wig, false eyelashes, a lot of badly applied lipstick and wearing a black sequin dress.* "

Identity Crisis

When Michael Bolton came to Dublin, like most visiting American artists, he stayed in the Four Seasons Hotel. On one particular night he was craving a veal parmigiana but didn't want to eat in the hotel restaurant – he wanted the meal prepared in an Italian restaurant. The concierge made several frantic phone calls, and within minutes the Town Bar and Grill restaurant had obliged. I happened to be dining there that night and that's how I know. I had also met and interviewed him earlier that day.

The interview had gone well. He was polite, engaging and extremely dishy. I was never a fan of 'big hair' for men, and when I saw that he had just moved from the eighties to the noughties by trading his mullet for a short back and sides, I was pleasantly surprised. This is a man who counts both *Desperate Housewives* stars Teri Hatcher and Nicollette Sheridan among his ex-partners, and I could now see the appeal. He has also raised in excess of $4 million for the charity he founded in 1993.

He was a nice guy, and although he didn't make me laugh (what's he doing in this chapter then, I hear you ask), it was to be our third meeting later that same day that amused me.

I left the restaurant to call in to the Four Seasons (another coincidence – I promise I wasn't stalking him, though I'm sure he thought I was) to meet my uncle Peter, who was visiting from California. Uncle Peter (who is actually my uncle-in-law) is a larger-than-life character who left Ireland in the 1950s, built a successful business and in his retirement returns home every summer for a month-long party.

As we were sitting in the hotel bar chatting, Michael Bolton arrived back from the restaurant, spotted me and came over to say hi.

'I'd like to introduce you to my uncle, Peter Devlin,' I said.

They shook hands and chatted for a few minutes. Uncle Peter asked how the concerts were going, told him he was a big fan and that he had seen him perform in his adopted hometown of Long Beach. Michael seemed flattered and they continued to shoot the breeze for a while.

When the conversation came to a close, Michael politely shook Uncle Peter's hand and said, 'Well, it was a pleasure meeting you, I hope you have a great trip.'

Uncle Peter then replied sincerely, 'And a pleasure meeting you too. It's such a pity that my wife Miriam and my two girls aren't here. When I get back to California, they're going to be so jealous that I came all the way to Dublin and met Kenny G.'

I couldn't believe it. I was mortified.

I looked at Michael with an apologetic grin. I was speechless. I'm not sure if it was out of embarrassment or annoyance, but Michael realised it would probably be better if he said nothing, apart from 'goodnight' as he walked away.

'Uncle Peter, that was Michael Bolton,' I said.

Unperturbed, Uncle Peter replied, 'Really? Jeez, he looks just like Kenny G.'

This is a man who counts both Desperate Housewives stars Teri Hatcher and Nicollette Sheridan among his ex-partners.

PJ Gallagher

PJ Gallagher is one of the most exciting new comedians to come out of Ireland in the last 10 years. His *Naked Camera* show has won an IFTA award and sales of the DVD have reached triple platinum. His most famous character is undoubtedly Jake Stevens, the most irritating, newspaper-waving, tuneless-whistling moron you're ever likely to meet. Unfortunately for me, I met him when PJ was filming his first-ever series, so I had no idea who this character was.

The *Big Brother* auditions had come to Dublin and I was covering the event for *Entertainment News*. I was interviewing hopeful contestants in the queue outside Dublin's RDS and a hidden camera crew was filming Jake. He approached me and told me he had what it takes to make it into the *Big Brother* house and that I should interview him now before he became a household name. I humoured him, as he was one of many overly confident and slightly unstable individuals present that day. The more he talked, the more I thought, 'Oh God, we have a complete lunatic here.' He ranted for ages, danced, strutted, whistled, sang and entertained everyone around him. I had no idea I was also being filmed by his hidden cameras, so thankfully I grinned and endured it.

When I was leaving later, someone from their production company approached and explained what they were doing. They asked me to sign a release form agreeing to be included in the show, which I gladly did. The show aired, and although I had expected to feel a little uncomfortable or slightly embarrassed, I think I got away lightly. Maybe the edit was kind, but it taught me to always be on guard – you never know when Big Brother is watching!

Irish
Pop-arrazi

Irish music has had many international successes over the years, both with traditional acts like The Chieftans and Clannad and with rock acts like Thin Lizzy, Rory Gallagher and U2, but it wasn't until the mid 1990s that Irish pop music finally began to make an impression around the world. Some bands came and went faster than B*witched could sing 'C'est La Vie', but others proved the begrudging Irish music press wrong by having hits, longevity and against all the odds, credibility. I'm an unashamed fan of Irish pop music and I also happen to be a fan of some of the people who make it.

Pop-ular Guy

There was a vicious rumour spread by jealous media types that Louis Walsh would fake phone calls from A-list celebs to his mobile anytime he was in a meeting.

I never really bought into it. On many occasions when I was having lunch, dinner or drinks with Louis we were interrupted (usually during the juiciest of gossip) by calls from people like Joan Rivers, Sharon Osbourne and Simon Cowell. On one occasion we were in the company of an Irish journalist when Louis's mobile rang. He answered and a few seconds later cupped his hand over the phone and whispered to us, 'Kate Moss.' He took the call outside and the journalist said, 'Do you really think it's her?'

'Yes, why not?'

'You don't think he's making it up?'

'Hardly. Why would he do that?'

Louis came back in and explained that Kate had invited him to a party.

He put his phone down on the table, excused himself and went to the loo. While he was gone, the journalist (who will remain nameless to protect the guilty) picked up Louis's phone to check his call log. I was very uncomfortable with this and all too aware that Louis knew the staff in the restaurant very well. If they saw what was going on, they would be sure to tell him. The curious hack found the number of the last call received. It was indeed from a London phone and he scribbled it down in his notebook just before Louis returned.

Later that day, the journalist sent me a text: 'It checked out – I have Kate Moss's number if you ever need it.'

'No thanks,' I replied. I knew that if I ever did need Kate Moss's number, all I would have to do is ask Louis.

Louis is quintessentially a nice guy who helps out those he likes and trusts. Yes, he occasionally loses the run of himself when he's caught up in *X Factor* superstardom, but after a few weeks back on Irish soil he reverts to character – slagging, teasing and generally giving those around him the same hard time he was given during his struggle to the top. As one of Ireland's most successful and now most famous music moguls, he remains admirably grounded.

My dad has known Louis longer than I have, as they have both been in the music business in Ireland since the early 1970s. Louis learned his trade booking and promoting show bands around the ballrooms and dancehalls of Ireland. My dad

> *It checked out – I have Kate Moss's number if you ever need it.*

With some of The Indians showband – Chris Mullahy, Brian Woodfull and my dad Eamonn (on the right)

remembers Louis as a very hard worker, determined that some day he would hit the big time managing a successful band.

In 1980, he convinced Irish singer Johnny Logan to enter the National Song Contest, then the Eurovision Song Contest, which he went on to win in front of a television audience of 500 million viewers.

Louis was up and running. Thirteen years later, he held auditions for a boy band and created Boyzone. Always able to create a media event when there was little or no story, the auditions got national media coverage and the winning line-up was offered a now-infamous appearance on *The Late Late Show*. The band broke the UK market and went on to sell over 12 million albums worldwide, which meant bigger doors were now open to Louis and his stable of artists.

He signed Westlife to RCA London having been impressed by their A&R executive, Simon Cowell. Louis liked Cowell's hands-on approach to the selection of songs and producers and a fruitful working relationship and friendship was born.

To this day there is loyalty and respect between the two men. Louis has assembled many bands for Simon, who then helps find the songs and advises on the music, and Simon has chosen many songs for Louis's acts which have gone on to be number one hits. Simon and Louis are a good team – they work well together, and more importantly, they trust each other in what's a very cutthroat, fickle business.

Simon obviously appreciates this, as he brought Louis with him to the phenomenal success that is *X Factor*. This has proven not only to be good for Louis's bank balance (on series three he told me he was earning £500,000 sterling for his part in the

> *Simon and Louis are a good team – they work well together, and more importantly, they trust each other in what's a very cutthroat, fickle business.*

show), but also for his profile in the UK. The young boy from Kiltamagh in County Mayo has done better than good.

When I started in TV3, Louis gave me a pretty tough time (see the Bee Gees story pp. 11–13), but it was all good-natured taunting and teasing. Slowly he came to realise that either I wasn't going away or that I may be of some use to him, because after a while we became friends.

> *In an attempt to protect our friendship by trying to pull a potentially damaging story, I almost lost my job for Louis.*

I'd like to think he respected the fact that I was just doing what he had done – working hard, doing my best and not taking it all too seriously. He became a valuable contact in the business and helped me any time he could. That meant getting me access to bands (not only his own), putting me in touch with celebrities and agents, especially in the UK (Louis has a pretty impressive contacts book), setting up interviews, coming out to TV3 with a minute's notice to do a live interview in studio with me because I had been let down by someone else, turning up at the launch of *Xposé* (and other TV3 events) to do photographs with me and making sure his bands gave me exclusive access all areas when on tour. Whatever I call asking for, Louis always does his best to help.

Of course, I try to reciprocate when I can and have plugged numerous new band launches and single and album releases and promoted tours when ticket sales were a little slow. But in an attempt to protect our friendship by trying to pull a potentially damaging story, I almost lost my job for Louis. Looking back, it seems rather pointless now, as the band in question lasted less than a year, but I was trying to be professional and do the honourable thing. My boss didn't see it that way though, and for different reasons, neither did Louis.

RTÉ ran a reality TV show to find the members of what would hopefully become Ireland's newest pop sensation, a band named Six. When the singers had been chosen, they were to make their first public appearance at Dublin's Mansion House and I went along to cover the story. Louis had set up a one-on-one interview with the band after the performance of their debut single. For the performance, my cameraman got permission to take an audio feed from

Pop-ular guy, Louis!

the sound desk, but for some reason he got the wrong mix and ended up recording the band's live mics instead. How this happened is beyond me. As is the norm with a lot of manufactured pop (and rock) bands these days, they were miming. That in itself seemed ridiculous, as all the band members had been chosen for their vocal abilities and had been filmed over eight weeks singing live on the TV show. Unfortunately for one of the vocalists, they were singing into a mic that was plugged into the desk (and then into our camera), but they weren't able to hear their own voice as there were no live vocals mixed in with the track. It wasn't until we got back to base and put the tapes into the editing machine that we realised what had happened. Kyle Anderson was singing at the top of his voice and sounded awful. It was funny, but it would have been unfair to broadcast it. Anyone trying to sing to a backing track without being able to hear their own voice is likely to be out of tune.

With the group Six, winners of Ireland's first reality talent series, Popstars

My superiors, however, decided that this was the story – 'Pop stars' show a farce! Louis's band can't sing after all!'

I begged TV3 not to run with this angle on the story, explaining that firstly it was untrue (Kyle probably had one of the best voices in the band, as seen by thousands of viewers on the TV show); secondly, it was unethical (our cameraman admitted it was our mistake by plugging into the wrong output of the desk); and thirdly, it would most likely mean the end of a very valuable (for the station) relationship with Louis Walsh.

'Please, look at the bigger picture. It's not worth losing Louis as a friend and contact just for one lame story.'

My pleas fell on deaf ears. I was told to write the piece, voice it and put my name to it. I refused. I was cautioned. I refused again. I was told it could cost me my job.

I did it, reluctantly, but I also phoned Louis and told him what was about to happen. He went ballistic! As expected, he told me if I didn't get the story pulled he would never deal with me or TV3 again. One last-ditch attempt with my boss failed again. In fact, it caused me even more trouble, as I was reprimanded 'for contacting Louis'. I argued that this was proper journalistic practice – a right to reply, so to speak.

The piece was aired, with my name attached. I stormed out of the newsroom in tears and returned to my desk the following day to find a formal written warning from TV3 waiting for me. A meeting with Personnel spelled out just how seriously they were taking the whole thing and it was explained to me that the incident had been noted on my file. (I received a similar letter about a year later when a photograph of Gráinne Seoige and myself appeared in a Sunday newspaper. She had invited me, as a friend, to the launch of Sky News Ireland, where she had just been appointed news anchor. As is the case with most presenters who leave TV3, she is persona non grata and to be seen to fraternise with such 'scoundrels' at a competitor's event was taken as some sort of act of betrayal.)

In the six months that followed, Louis, true to his word, refused to deal with TV3 no matter how hard I tried. After much persistence I convinced him to meet me for coffee and brought a copy of the written warning TV3 had given to me. He couldn't believe it. He respected that I had put my neck on the line for him and realised that there were certain decisions that were out of my hands. He agreed to forget the whole episode, and before long we were planning our next story.

Boyz to Gentlemen

The thing that always struck me about Boyzone, and I've spent a lot of time with the lads, is that they always genuinely seemed to be having fun. They never took themselves or the band too seriously. It's probably what led to their break-up, in fact – none of them realised just how big they were and what they had achieved until it was gone.

Their reunion has changed all that, and now, with Stephen gone, I don't think they'll ever take success or each other for granted again.

From my point of view, working with a group who was having fun made the job much easier. I got to be there when they were making music videos, rehearsing in dance studios, singing in recording studios, waiting in their dressing rooms, backstage, onstage, side of stage, on the tour bus, in hotels and in their homes. Off camera we met up at dinner parties, fundraising lunches and charity balls, and I have witnessed their less-than-professional performances on the football pitch and the golf course. I don't think I've ever refused an invitation to be with any of the lads and I never will. They're

A shot taken in the Boyzone dressing room on one of their earlier tours

always full of energy and fun to be around – the teasing and slagging is incessant and I hope that never changes.

I quickly found out that no matter how much you prepared for a Boyzone interview or how much you tried to steer the conversation in one direction, inevitably you had to give up and go with the flow. Once they started, it was difficult to get them to stop. If we were on location and there were no time constraints, this would often mean arriving back to the studio with enough footage for a full-length documentary – an editor's nightmare.

Speaking of nightmares, I remember going up to Belfast for the Boyzone reunion tour. Louis had assured me I would have access all areas, as usual. It was a Sunday night, but as it was the first night of their tour, it was an event worth covering. My cameraman, Alan, was new on the job and very excited to be filming a piece for *Entertainment News*. He had spent his previous (first) week hanging around the Dublin courts in miserable weather. This was going to be a lot more exciting, especially as his girlfriend was a huge fan of the band. I promised her an autographed photo.

With Bruce Willis at the opening of Planet Hollywod in Dublin

> He revealed some very intimate details about his relationship with ex-wife Liza Minelli and her problems with alcohol addiction.

my single crew cameraman, David with his production team of eight. We both kept filming and an introduction and chat followed that was recorded by both cameras. I asked him a few questions and he seemed very forthcoming, so I suggested we do a proper interview in the Westlife dressing room. He agreed and I ended up getting a bonus interview for our first *Xposé* show.

He revealed some very intimate details about his relationship with ex-wife Liza Minelli and her problems with alcohol addiction. TV3 chose not to air the more graphic revelations for fear of legal action. He painted a very grim picture of her mental and physical health, and coming from David Gest, I found that to be pretty shocking.

A deafening roar from front of stage meant that lights were down and the show was about to start. I left David and ran to the side of stage to see and film the start of the show.

When you're meeting celebrities every day, sometimes you forget just how special and talented they can be. When you get a chance to see them in action, up close and in front of their audience, it really is a pleasure – probably the most enjoyable part of the job. Seeing and hearing thousands of screaming, adoring fans reminds me why we're there in the first place and how hard these guys work not just to get to where they are, but to maintain their level of success.

It was, as always, a spectacular show, but after five songs we knew we had to pack up and get on the road home to Dublin. It was going to be a late night and I knew I would have a very early start the following day. I would have to script, edit and voice the Westlife package and the David Gest interview before even thinking about presenting the first *Xposé* show.

Home

Most of us like to see how the other half lives, and when I've been lucky enough to get access to celebrities' homes, it generally makes for a better interview. They feel more comfortable and more relaxed in their own place and tend to let their guard down a little. It's also nice to have a nose through the keyhole, isn't it?

When Westlife played their first homecoming concert in Mark, Shane and Kian's hometown of Sligo, I was invited to Shane's house for a pre-gig interview. Himself and Gillian had just finished building a luxurious new five-bedroom detached home and welcomed me with my crew and outside broadcasting unit. The OBU is basically a bread van with a satellite dish stuck on the roof. It looked a little unsightly parked in the driveway, but the hospitable couple didn't mind, as we needed it for our live link-up to studio.

The shot was set up at Shane's grand piano in the hallway of the house and it was agreed that just he and I would do the interview. The rest of the band retired to the TV room to watch a golf tournament, and before long the cameraman gave us the cue that we were live. All was going well until Brian McFadden, ever the joker, appeared in front of us but behind the camera and out of shot.

Hanging out at Shane's house

In an attempt to put us off, make us laugh and entertain the others, he dropped his trousers, right in front of us, midway through one of my questions.

In an attempt to put us off, make us laugh and entertain the others, he dropped his trousers, right in front of us, midway through one of my questions. To say I lost my train of thought would be an understatement. Both Shane and myself started laughing and I quickly realised I had to let the viewer in on the joke. I told the cameraman to turn the camera around. As he lifted it from the tripod, Brian panicked, and in an attempt to simultaneously pull up his trousers and exit the room, he fell over. The tables were well and truly turned and the audience got to see a side of Brian they had previously never seen. Shane and myself did our best to continue the interview, but I knew I had more than enough (literally) of Westlife for my broadcast. You just can't beat live TV!

Saying Goodbye to Brian

A press release was issued by Westlife's management and sent to every newsroom in the country, stating Westlife had an announcement to make and that a press conference was to be held in Dublin's Four Seasons Hotel at 12 noon the following day. All members of the band would be present and available for comment then, but not before. There was a lot of rumour and speculation, the most common being that they were splitting up.

I rang Louis.

'I can't say anything. That's why we're having a press conference, Lorraine. You'll have to wait.'

I had expected that answer, but it wasn't what I wanted to hear. I wanted to break the story, exclusively, that evening on *TV3 News*. I kept at him.

'Come on, Louis. You know what this would mean to me. We always help each other out.' I was relentless, and finally, much to my surprise and delight, he gave in. He told me Brian was leaving the band.

I couldn't believe it. This was not what anyone expected. I ran with the story on the 5:30 news bulletin. Immediately after the broadcast, the phones started hopping.

Irish and UK media wanted to know for sure if what I had reported was true. Of course it was, but I couldn't reveal my source. All I could say was, 'A source very, very, very close to the band has confirmed to me that Brian is leaving.' *GMTV* contacted me. Would I be interested in going live into the show the following morning? It meant being dolled up and ready to go live from the Four Seasons Hotel at 6 a.m., but hey, it was a massive audience across Ireland and the UK, so it was well worth an earlier-than-normal start. TV3 gave me the go-ahead on the basis that I was 'strapped' (the title under my name when it came on screen) and introduced as TV3's Entertainment Correspondent.

I arrived at the Four Seasons at 5:45 a.m. on a bitterly cold winter morning with hair and make-up done and lines rehearsed. It was my first time working with *GMTV*, so I wanted to get it right. I went live shortly after 6:30 a.m. with Eamonn Holmes. They liked it and asked me to go again just after 7 a.m., again with Penny at 8 a.m. and finally with Lorraine Kelly at 9 a.m.

One of my favourite Westlife pics

After what seemed like a full day's broadcasting, I went straight to our studios in Ballymount to do a bit of prep before heading back to the Four Seasons for the official press conference.

By now, all the press knew what the story was, but they still needed to get the line for themselves and the shots to go with it.

I'll never forget the press conference. Everyone was chatting loudly until the lads walked in, and to say their mood was sombre would be an understatement. They looked devastated. We knew they weren't breaking up, but could this signal the end for Westlife? Everyone was comparing it to the departure of Robbie Williams, something which Take That had, at that time, never recovered from. I genuinely felt sorry for all of them. Their futures hung in the balance.

When I talked to them shortly after, Kian, who had cried openly during the press conference, was annoyed with me. He and the rest of the band had watched my reports on *GMTV* and hadn't liked what I said about Westlife's future now being uncertain. I explained that when a founding member of any band leaves, no one can be sure how it will affect the remaining band members, or more importantly, how the fans will react. I offered him and the other three guys the opportunity to show a united front by going on camera and stating their intentions to carry on as a band.

They did and proved me wrong about the uncertainty of their future.

'Come on, Louis. You know what this would mean to me. We always help each other out.' I was relentless, and finally, much to my surprise and delight, he gave in. He told me Brian was leaving the band.

In my opening piece to camera outside Keith and Lisa's house in the bright sunshine, my newly self-designed knitted coat dress (which I had been keeping for a special occasion) was completely see-through. The frontal was wasn't too bad, as I was wearing a bra and that's all you could see, but when I turned around to walk into the house, my smalls (and boy, were they small) were there for all and sundry to see, along with a very untoned derriere!

There was nothing I could do. We recorded the show as live every day, just before broadcast, and as I had been late, there was no time for a rerun.

I could hear the entire gallery staff (the operators behind the scene) in convulsions of laughter. My producer tried to tell me it was fine in my earpiece, but I could see it very clearly. How did Keith, Lisa and the cameraman not notice? Maybe they had but chose not to say anything, which was even worse. To get through the rest of the show, I just thought about the message in the piece and recited my newly adopted mantra – 'don't sweat the small stuff'.

The first thing I did when I came out of studio was ring Keith.

'What did you think?'

'It was great, we both loved it.'

> *When I turned around to walk into the house, my smalls (and boy, were they small) were there for all and sundry to see, along with a very untoned derriere!*

With Keith and Lisa Duffy at Brown Thomas Autism Action Jimmy Choo event 2009

'But my underwear … did you see the G-string? What did Lisa say?'

'We didn't see a thing, honestly. Jesus, we would've told you if we'd noticed.'

'So it must have just been the glaring sunlight then?'

'Yes, stop worrying. I'm sure no one else noticed it. You're just being paranoid.'

He was wrong. The phones in the office started ringing with irate viewers (mostly women) complaining about their families having to look at my uncovered rear as they were trying to eat their dinner. My saving grace was that none of the press decided to pick up on the story – perhaps they weren't able to reproduce the images well enough to print. On my website, stacpoolekeane.com, that dress carries a warning – 'May be see-through. Slip advised!'

Ronan's Gift!

Like Keith, I got to know Ronan through my charity work with his family. Along with his siblings, Ronan set up the Marie Keating Foundation in memory of their mother to provide life-saving breast cancer screening for women all over Ireland. It's an incredible charity, they've done tremendous work and I'm always delighted to help out any way I can, so our paths have crossed on a personal as well as professional level. To this end, I've also enjoyed working with Ronan's sister Linda, brother Gary and Gary's wife, Valerie.

Infidelities aside, Ronan has always been one of the good guys, grounded by his upbringing and very normal surroundings, family and friends. He's also a good sport, although I do remember that in the early days, Ronan Keating didn't like being the butt of one particular joke.

Ian Dempsey and Mario Rosenstock

Mario Rosenstock had introduced a Ronan character to his *Gift Grub* ensemble on the *Ian Dempsey Breakfast Show*, and like most parodies it was less than complimentary. Every sentence began with the words 'fair play' and ended with 'please God'. Ronan was not at all impressed with his doppelganger, mainly because it portrayed him as a bit of a gombeen. Mario told me that as a result, he refused to come on the show or have anything to do with Today FM.

Unfortunately for Ronan, the character was an extremely popular one, and along with (Radio) Roy Keane, Daniel

O'Donnell, Bertie and José Mourinho, he became a regular fixture in the sketches. The first time I mentioned it to Ronan, I knew I had touched on a sore point and made a mental note not to bring it up again.

Roll on a couple of years, and with a hugely successful solo career, an older and wiser Ronan was ready to see the funny side. *Gift Grub* album sales in Ireland were almost as high as his own, and when I broached the subject for the second time he was much more relaxed. He agreed to be filmed reading the same 'Radio Ro' script as Mario, as a double act for my TV cameras.

We went to the Today FM studios in the morning and recorded one of the sketches with Mario, and Ronan later repeated the lines for Sybil and our cameras from his home studio. We were able to cut between the two, comparing voices, and it made for a great piece of TV. It also endeared Ronan more to our audience, and not that he needed to, but to me also. 'Love Me for a Reason'? I'll give you three – good looking, talented and a sense of humour!

Teddy bears at the Picnic
– the animals invade the
Flaming Lips stage

Having an access all areas pass means I can watch the bands from side of stage, which is one of the perks of the job for me. One of my favourite bands, The Flaming Lips, was headlining the main stage and myself and my friend Ali were there for the duration. Near the end of the set, a large group of people started gathering beside us at the side of the stage. A roadie started passing out costumes to those who were obviously going to play a part in the live show. As they all started to get dressed up, he handed us two oversized animal costumes and shouted over the music, 'Put them on!'

'What?' we shouted back.

'Quick, get dressed, you're on after this song.'

He obviously thought we were part of the crew, but being a huge fan (and having consumed a few beers – I deserved them, I had been working all day!), I couldn't let the opportunity pass. Before long, Ali and I were jumping around the stage, dancing with lead singer Wayne Coyne and waving to the 20,000-strong crowd. I have never experienced an adrenalin rush like it (well, apart from my New York rooftop moment with Bono), but being able to see your audience instead of just reading about them in the Neilson TV ratings is incredible. I should've stuck with the singing lessons…

When Ryan Crossed the Line

'I should have paid more attention in political history class,' I'd said to Ryan Tubridy the following year.

It was the day after his first ever *Late Late Show* (remember the Brian Cowen interview?) and myself, Ryan, his girlfriend Aoibhinn, our agent Noel Kelly and his wife Catriona had all travelled down to the Electric Picnic together. Peter, a die-hard 'Picnicker', had pitched up a day earlier. The mood was celebratory, to say the least. There had been a party after the show, and as we read the newspapers on the way down the consensus was that it had been a resounding success for Ryan.

Probably the last thing Ryan wanted to do was travel to a festival to work, but he had a long-standing engagement to host a talk show/debate of sorts in the 'Mind Field' area. En route he got the news that one of his guests had pulled out at the last minute and asked me if I would stand in. He promised me it wouldn't be too taxing on our

At Electric Picnic with Ryan Tubridy, John Snow and Mark Little

already tired and hungover brains, so I reluctantly agreed on the condition that he would go easy on me.

As he introduced the panel, I had the terrible realisation that I'd been duped. 'Please welcome onto the stage Miss Lorraine Keane, Mark Little from *Primetime* and John Snow from *Channel 4 News*!' Oops. Talk about being out of your depth. There I was, sitting beside two of the finest political commentators on television, and I hadn't so much as read a newspaper in days.

Then the dreaded debate began. As Ryan paced the stage, still feeling euphoric, triumphant and maybe even a little bit tipsy from the night before, he announced, 'And my first question goes to Lorraine Keane.'

Dread and fear.

'Lorraine, do you want *The Afternoon Show* on RTÉ and did you leave *Xposé* because it's impossible to work in an office full of bitches? Discuss!'

A loud cheer went up from the packed marquee. Part of me was elated that he hadn't asked me for a solution to the political failure in the Israeli-Palestinian conflict, but I was also just a little bit miffed that he got one over on me, set me up (onstage!) and was now able to sit back and have a good laugh at my expense.

I answered as best I could, and was explaining how well we girls got on together when a female voice shouted out, 'Liar!' A sharp intake of breath from the crowd and a convivial 'Bitch!' reply from me just stoked the fire for our host. Ryan rooted her out, got her onstage and a full-blown debate followed about ruthless ambition and bitchiness in the workplace and whether an office of males was more dangerous than an office full of females (Mark Little argued that an office full of male journalists was by far the worst).

When Ryan tried to move on to the serious subjects, John Snow interrupted: 'I'd like to hear more about this *Xposé* show with all these glamorous girls who may or may not get on together, it sounds fascinating.'

The conversation did become fascinating as soon as John and Mark started discussing American foreign policy, the future of Ireland's economy and comparing the Clintons and the Obamas, among many other various topics.

The show ended up being great fun and it was a pleasure to share the stage with three such wonderful characters. As soon as we had finished, we couldn't get to the bar quick enough, where Mr Tubridy bought the drinks as a peace offering.

> "'Lorraine, do you want The Afternoon Show on RTÉ and did you leave Xposé because it's impossible to work in an office full of bitches? Discuss!'"

You Can't Be My Hero, Baby

The Meteor Awards ceremony is always a great event, particularly when the music ends and the offstage antics begin. There was Caprice's VPL (visible panty line), Samantha Mumba's 'wardrobe malfunction' and Snoop Dogg drooling over Glenda Gilson and resorting to smoking his roll-your-own cones in Spirit nightclub when she told him she wasn't interested. Who could forget Louis Walsh grabbing Kerry Katona from behind where he shouldn't have and Brian McFadden defending Delta's honour when another entourage pushed her out of the way? The backstage shenanigans would certainly give the main show a run for its money if the cameras were allowed to roll.

For me, though, the lowlight of a decade of the Meteors was when Enrique Iglesias stood me up. Yes, the incredibly handsome Spanish singer was due to co-present an award with me one year, but after his musical performance informed organisers that he was just 'too horny' to hang about. He decided not to be my hero, baby, jumped on his private jet back to London and left me to go solo.

I might not have scored with Enrique, but I did manage to score a gong, albeit by default. Kathryn Thomas and I were asked by Meteors organiser Caroline Downey to present the Best Band award at the 2010 Meteors. The presentation took place late in the evening and we were both too distracted (they were serving cocktails in the backstage bar) to prepare anything in the way of an intro or even rehearse who would say what onstage. We made our way through the nominees, showed the clip and announced the winner – Snow Patrol. Unfortunately, the band was in LA but appeared onscreen with a pre-recorded thank you. I was left holding their award, and as I walked offstage I asked where I should leave it. 'Just take it with you,' the stage manager said, so I took the trophy back to the bar where the party was continuing, with the intention of giving it to Caroline Downey.

> *I might not have scored with Enrique, but I did manage to score a gong, albeit by default.*

When I arrived into the VIP room, award in hand, there was great excitement. A queue started to form for photos. We set up mock presentations and photo opportunities for friends of ours who had lost out on awards that night. But by the time the award had been photographed more times than the event had nominees

About 40 minutes later, Mel Gibson and I shared the most delicious plate of fish and chips (the waiter provided plates and cutlery) while a horde of hungry VIPs looked on enviously.

Through mouthfuls of salty chips we managed a chat about family holidays, working in Ireland and his delight at being back here. I found him to be a charming gentleman, nothing like the drunken, violent racist he has been portrayed as in the media.

Back in the corner of the room, our cosy table for four was being swamped by every beautiful young thing in the building, and it wasn't my husband they were after. The Chablis was kicking in and the girls were getting braver. Peter was being approached by people he barely knew with a 'Hi, Peter, how are you, won't you introduce me to your friend?' I could tell that John Corbett seemed to be enjoying all the attention (the Guinness wasn't the only thing going to his head) while Bo Derek was definitely not.

After several attempts she managed to pry him away from his adoring fans, who by now resembled a line of pre-teens at a Jedward record signing.

He and Peter swapped numbers before they left, and as they scribbled digits onto beer mats I couldn't help noticing at least a dozen pairs of eyes straining to catch a glimpse of what was being written.

As we left the Shelbourne that night, I asked my 'reluctant to come to any event' husband the rhetorical question, 'So, was *that* worth putting on a suit for?'

'It was definitely one of the better ones,' he said with a smile.

We had been in the car less than a minute and I hadn't even put my seat belt on when Peter announced to the driver, 'Fran, you'll never guess who gave me a lift to the party tonight.'

I still haven't heard the end of it.

Mel Gibson

One Is Keane on You

I've written about many people who made a lasting impression on me, but I'm told that there are those who I made a lasting impression on too, although if I'm honest, as with the earlier example of Miss Hayes, sometimes it was for the wrong reasons. I'm not sure if it was down to nerves or just an unhappy coincidence, but most of my encounters with presidents, prime ministers and royalty had their fair share of hiccups.

In the case of Prince Charles, I was flattered and honoured to be asked to introduce him at the opening of Angels Quest respite home in Glenageary, County Dublin. It was his first visit to the Republic, so it meant there was huge interest from a media perspective. The charity's founder, Deirdre Kelly, asked me to say a few words of welcome before the introduction, so I put a lot of preparation into my speech in the days leading up to the event. I chose my wardrobe (a green blouse from Irish label Regine and jewels borrowed from Appleby) as carefully as my words. On the day, I made sure to be there a couple of hours in advance, as I knew traffic and security around the venue would be plentiful and also because I wanted some time for a run-through.

In hindsight, that was probably my downfall. I had so much time that I became completely engrossed in a conversation with some of the children in the home. I totally lost track of time, and when it was my turn to kick off proceedings, I didn't even hear my cue. On his arrival, Prince Charles walked the meet and greet line of dignitaries, special guests and staff of the home. While I was on my hunkers chatting away to the children in the far corner of the room, my name was called. I wasn't paying attention and continued chatting. I was called again. Still nothing. One of the volunteers spotted me, ran over and gave me a nudge. I jumped up and pushed myself quickly and apologetically through the

> *In a most perfect Bridget Jones moment, I tripped over the cables, stumbled and, to the gasps of the crowd, landed with one knee on the ground, the other leg stretched behind me and my head no less than an inch from His Royal Highness's crotch!*

crowd towards the waiting prince and podium. As I got closer I realised that I hadn't done my run-through, I'd forgotten to check protocol – should I curtsy or shake his hand – and worst of all, I had forgotten my notes. Oh, and insignificant as it may seem, I had also forgotten to check my hair and make-up and touch up my lipstick. Disaster. Distracted by my thoughts and in a serious panic as I rushed to the stage, I didn't notice the large black TV cables in front of the podium which had been installed after I arrived. In a most perfect

With Michael Martin TD, Mary Hanafin TD, Deirdre Kelly and Prince Charles

Bridget Jones moment, I tripped over the cables, stumbled and, to the gasps of the crowd, landed with one knee on the ground, the other leg stretched behind me and my head no less than an inch from His Royal Highness's crotch! I can only compare my entrance to a charging rhinoceros who changed his mind at the last minute and genuflected.

There were a few sniggers, followed by a very uncomfortable silence.

I took a deep breath, regained my composure, smiled and said, 'I can't believe I was worried about protocol.' I heard a few laughs and a collective sigh of relief.

After that entrance, I didn't need my notes and just decided to ad lib. I got through my introduction and welcome speech with a little more grace and dignity. Chatting

Ronan Keating and Prince Charles

to Prince Charles later, he said, 'I believe you are involved in television.'

'Yes, although I'm usually the one covering entertainment rather than providing it,' I said.

'And are you working today?'

'No, thanks to you I have the day off!'

'Well, I am delighted to see I am good for something.'

A royal with a sense of humour – who'd have thunk it?

Taoiseach Can Take a Joke

Outside the offices of the Dáil one evening, a TV3 reporter asked Bertie Ahern for a comment on the *Gift Grub* sketches lampooning him on an almost daily basis. 'Bertie the chef' was the first of many popular characters devised by Mario Rosenstock for *Ian Dempsey's Breakfast Show* on Today FM, and his catchphrases, such as 'ye spanner', 'infacta' and 'jaysus', were becoming part of the vernacular. The Taoiseach (he was leader at the time) diplomatically explained that he had not heard the sketches and therefore could not make any comment. He got into his waiting car as the reporter turned off his camera and put away his microphone.

Instead of driving straight out the gate, the Taoiseach's car changed course and pulled up beside my TV3 colleague. As his driver slowed down, Bertie rolled down the window and leaning out of the car, shouted, 'Go on, ye spanner!'

A politician with a sense of humour? Now, more than ever, we need more of those!

Bertie rolled down the window and leaning out of the car, shouted, 'Go on, ye spanner!'

With Bertie Ahern

·Ready
for my
Close-up·

I love fashion. My mum says I had an interest in style from a very early age. I spent my communion money on shoes and my confirmation money on a ra ra skirt and matching blouse (it was the 1980s, give me a break!). Roll on my first real paycheque – a mere £300 per month as a reporter at AA Roadwatch – of which I spent £250 on a pair of thigh-high black Prada boots from Brown Thomas. The remaining £50 went to my mum, which she had to give back to me for bus fare to get me into work until my next paycheque (in exchange for an IOU, of course). I couldn't afford to go out for the following four weeks, but I had the boots. They were too good to wear to work (I worked on radio), so I wore them around the house every evening. They were well broken in by the time they had their first public outing. It was worth the sacrifice! I still have those boots. They are still perfect and I still wear them.

There are worse things to be motivated by, I guess. The only harm my fashion fixation causes is to my bank balance. With four younger sisters and two daughters, I can convince myself that most of my purchases are long-term investments, one day to become hand-me-downs, or if I'm overly optimistic, heirlooms. Think vintage, darling!

It's also a part of the job I take a lot of pride in. I've been told many times by women that they'd only tune in to see what I was wearing. I was always very conscious of this – in over 500 TV shows, I never wore the same thing twice! If you can get people to tune in for whatever the reason and if they like what they see, they may stay watching and tune in again. I always left my wardrobe credit until last, and I decided to do the same with this book.

Getting ready for an awards show, red carpet event or cover shoot is probably the most fun of all, not least because my 'A Team' of little sisters, Tori Keane on hair and Becky Keane on make-up, are always with me (I love these girls), but the fuss, the buzz and the fun are also addictive.

To be honest, a fashion chapter was extremely difficult to put together. For a start, there's enough material to fill an entire book on that subject alone, and secondly, how do you select a bunch of photos of yourself in different ensembles at different events without having it look like a big Lorraine love-in? The answer is, you don't – you get your girlfriends, sisters and mother to choose them for you.

Fortunately, these fabulous women know me well enough to be truly honest and have included some of my fashion faux pas, just in case you missed them the first time around. A drawback of the day job is that when you get it wrong, you're photographed for all and sundry to see. I've had my fair share of delusional moments – enjoy them!

I love this dress. It was designed by Marion Murphy Cooney for the 2008 IFTAs. The gorgeous Rene Russo (who was wearing my second favourite dress on the night, a Roberto Cavalli nude silk dress) actually stopped me before I left the party to tell me that mine was her favourite and enquired where she could get one. Result!

Irish design duo Tanem Michael had designed some fabulous red dresses for an Xposé photo shoot months earlier, but they were never used in the poster campaign. It was a real shame, so I asked them to design my dress for the 2009 VIP Style Awards. I won that year, so I was delighted they got the exposure they deserved in the end. As always, my stylist sisters, Tori and Becky, did my hair and make-up and were my dates on the night.

I was handing over the tiara at the 2010 VIP Style Awards, so I decided to go simple in this Alex Perry (from Sydney, Australia) blush chiffon dress. My accessories are from costume jewellery house Gemini Jewellery and my bag is from Top Shop accessorised with a Gemini brooch.

I love lace, and one of my favourite designers, Marion Murphy Cooney from Nenagh in County Tipperary, created this bronze lace dress for the 2008 VIP Style Awards. I discovered Marion a few years earlier at a fundraising fashion show in Adare Manor, where she was showing one of her first 'ready to wear' collections. I borrowed most of it for a VIP cover shoot I was doing a few weeks later and a friendship was born. The lace looks antique but it was actually bought from Hickeys, where I buy most of my fabric. The neckline suits me because I have a small, narrow figure. I never wear a different colour on top and bottom because I'm too short. One colour makes me look longer and leaner. Pictured here with Blathnaid Ni Chofaigh and Laura Woods.

This dress is also by Marion Murphy Cooney for the 2007 VIP Style Awards. It's my favourite colour. Marion added the little brooch to the waistband. Both it and my jewellery are from Gemini Jewellery.

Deborah Veale and I at the Irish Tatler Women of the Year Awards 2009. My dress is Julia Clancey from Caru.

Tori gave me big hair for the 2008 Irish Tatler Women of the Year Awards and Alex Perry designed this dress for me. He designed a similar dress for Penelope Cruz.

With the 2006 VIP Style Award winner, Pamela Flood. I won this beautiful Appleby diamond necklace for being the 'Best Dressed' on the night, wearing a dress by Marion Murphy Cooney. It was also my birthday and I was three months pregnant, so I had lots to celebrate.

Thank goodness one of my favourite designers, Deborah Veale, is also one of my best friends and my neighbour. Never very organised, I came home from France the day of the awards with nothing to wear and headed straight over to Deborah's studio to try on a dress. This was just perfect and fit like a glove. It's one of my favourite pieces in my wardrobe now. Paul Sheeran lent me the jewellery to finish the look.

Pictured at the O₂ Ability Awards with Ryan and Clare. This is a dress by Irish design duo Kate&Ava. I was the first to put their collection on television and they're now stocked in boutiques nationwide. They're the best thing to come out of the Irish fashion industry in the last few years.

Jedward were particularly taken with my Alexander McQueen skull ring clutch.

I hosted the TV Now Awards for the first time in 2008, along with Diarmuid Gavin. I went to Sydney, Australia for this lemon chiffon gown, designed by Alex Perry, couturier to the stars. It's my favourite dress of all time – I even prefer it to my wedding dress. Alex hand dyed peacock feathers that he attached to the skirt with Swarovski crystals, which made it quite heavy. Unfortunately, it had been raining all day on the red carpet, so upon my arrival, when I let my train down for the photos, the peacock feathers got soaked. This not only made the dress even heavier, but it meant that every time I walked across the stage that night, I could feel soggy feathers sticking to the back of my legs – obviously a dress more suitable for an Australian climate. Alex Perry designs for Kylie and Danni Minogue, Nicole Kidman and Natalie Imbruglia.

As host of the TV Now Awards 2009, I got the opportunity to wear not one but two fabulous creations from Synan O'Mahony. Sy has been dressing me for over 10 years now. Described as Ireland's Ellie Saab, Synan is one of Ireland's best couturiers. I wore lavender and gold on the red carpet and blush and black for the ceremony. My sisters Tori and Becky were with me throughout the filming of the entire presentation (backstage), making sure I didn't have a hair or lip line out of place.

For the TV Now Awards 2007, I wore a dress from my own fashion label, Stacpoole & Keane. Michelina Stacpoole has been designing exquisite knitwear for 40 years in Ireland. We designed a small collection together for fun, for me to wear on TV. Shortly after, I was approached by people who wanted to buy the pieces, so we collaborated on two more collections together and hope to do more in the future.

I'm still not sure whether it was hormones or just a moment of madness, but I insisted Marion Murphy Cooney 'go short' for my 2006 TV Now Awards dress, and this revealing little number always comes back to haunt me. I had just discovered I was pregnant with my second child. I was over the moon, but also well aware that short skirts would not be playing a part in my wardrobe for some time to come. I also had a cleavage for the second time in my life (thanks to the hormones), which I was very proud of. One thing I had forgotten, however, was that the pregnancy process is a lot faster than the dressmaking process, and my growth from the first fitting to the last left me with a rather different physique. Not wanting to make me cry, on that final fitting just hours before the event, Marion did her best to nip and tuck my pride back into place. It worked and I thought I was fabulous (dam those hormones!). I even added a brooch to my hair that belonged to Granny Butler, my best friend's nan, for good luck. Taking to the red carpet, I was on top of the world (and a little top heavy to boot).

I'll never forget my father-in-law's comment a few years later when the photo reappeared in one of the papers: 'Merciful hour, what were you thinking? I'm not sure I was!

This photo was taken on my stairs before leaving the house on the night of the 2004 IFTAs. Synan O'Mahony designed this dress for me. The following year, Roberto Cavalli designed a very similar dress in blue and white for Victoria Beckham. Sy is always one step ahead in the style stakes.

This is a dress from one of my favourite Irish labels, Fran & Jane. At the 2009 Meteors I presented the award for Best Radio Show to Ray Foley at Today FM. The event organiser, the fabulous Caroline Downey, kindly arranged for Enrique Iglesias, who performed at the ceremony, to co-present the award with me. However, moments before we were due to go up on stage, he stated he was 'too horny and couldn't hang around' and left. A kiss from Ray Foley on stage went some way to making up for it!

Wearing my Fashion Targets Breast Cancer T-shirt with pride. I'm delighted to support FTBC in conjunction with Brown Thomas, the Irish Cancer Society and Europa Donna Ireland every year.

Like me, Ian Galvin eats, drinks and sleeps fashion. We are pictured at the Brown Thomas Autumn/Winter Collection Fashion Show 2009. I'm wearing a Manoush dress from BT2.

At the Brown Thomas/Jimmy Choo fundraiser for Autism Action, I'm wearing Jimmy Choo boots (designed especially for the event using Donegal Tweed) and a dress from Divine Boutique in Maynooth and Malahide.

I was delighted to support the launch of Paul Costelloe's jewellery range. He is as big in personality as he is in stature (6 feet 7 inches). My dress is from Divine Boutique and my jewellery and clutch are by London-based Russian designer, Lara Bohinc.

I prefer my back to my front, so this is one of my favourite dresses, by Antik Batik.

Myself and my fellow ex-AA Roadwatcher, Nuala Carey, at the 10th birthday celebrations of Karen Millen in Ireland. My dress is from Divine Boutique, my boots are Sergio Rossi from Fitzpatricks and my backpack is vintage Chanel.

Myself and Romy at Hamleys, Dundrum. I am wearing Lainey Keogh. Romy is wearing her favourite coat, from Petite in Dublin.

A great little dress that works as well in winter as in summer. Everything I'm wearing is from Seagreen, except my bag, which is Chanel.

This photo was taken at a dinner party in friends Norah Casey and Richard Hannaford's house. My dress is Marion Murphy Cooney and my shoes are Mathew Williamson at the Design Centre in Powerscourt. My plait is from Hairspray, Wicklow Street and Dundrum.

Amy Winehouse has this same dress. Preen only made three in this colour. I got the sample for the launch party of Xposé in City Hall in Dublin in 2007, when Louis Walsh came along to support me.

I bought this same dress in black, navy blue, lime green and coral. For the RTE Guide Christmas cover I'm wearing the navy Preen dress with Deborah Veale jewellery.

Happy days – me and the Xposé girls, a great bunch of gals, celebrating our first birthday at Krystle in 2008. This dress is also backless. The theme was red but I had no time to get a new red dress, so I improvised by sewing a red bow on the back.

With Cecilia Ahem and Yvonne Keating at Gerald Kean's Marie Antoinette-themed 50th birthday party. We are all wearing Synan O'Mahony creations. I gave Sy three days' notice for my dress, which he made out of leftover curtain and upholstery fabric I had in my attic. He is a genius!

I hosted the inaugural Dublin Fashion Week Awards ceremony in CHQ in Dublin, which showcased designs by Richard Lewis, John Rocha, Deborah Veale and Pauric Sweeney, amongst others. Richard Lewis made me this LGD (little grey dress) for the occasion. It needed nothing but a Chanel bag to top it off. I'm pictured here with Mary Andrews.

This is a backless David Szeto dress I bought in Harvey Nichols in Dundrum for the opening of the Annoushka jewellery boutique in Brown Thomas. Annoushka asked me to wear her jewellery that night at dinner. Annoushka, who was the creator/designer of Links of London, is still one of my designers of choice. I love the way she mixes and stacks all colours of metals and stones. I wore her pieces in a shoot and on the cover of Tatler magazine the following month. The collection was so valuable that it arrived at Barry and Mark McCall's studio with its own security guard, who watched over the pieces for the entire four-hour shoot. Now that's unbe-bling-able!

Wearing a Deborah Veale dress and Annoushka jewellery to present at the People of the Year Awards 2010 on RTÉ.

169

Shoes, glorious shoes… If I don't know what to wear, I start from the feet up, as shoes are my favourite fashion accessory. The secret is to know what suits you best. Just because something is fashionable doesn't mean you should wear it. The same applies to shoes. I have small feet (size 3 to 4) and I remember Robert O'Byrne telling me, 'Avoid round toes, darling, they will completely cut you off.' He's right – my feet are like full stops at the ends of my legs. Here, I'm pictured with Rachel Armstrong, the designer/buyer from Fitzpatricks Shoes in Dublin. Their own brand collection is as good as any Louboutin or Manolo, but at a third of the price. I'm also a big fan of Buffalo shoes – they're affordable, comfortable and always on trend. I even have a pair of shoes named after me, the Lolly Ks. SJP, eat your heart out!

At the Sex and the City 2 premiere in Harvey Nichols in Dundrum, wearing a Vivienne Westwood dress from Eden Boutique in Dundalk, a Chesneau handbag and Fitzpatricks shoes.

I'm delighted to be Ireland's first spokesperson for Garnier. At the photo call launch I wore a Roland Mouret dress from Costume in Dublin.

At the Alwear Autumn/Winter fashion show, wearing A wear.

This was taken for an 'at home' shoot I did for VIP magazine. I'm wearing one of my favourite labels, Anthology, from Avoca. It's one of the few labels that combines comfort and glamour perfectly, which means I can wear it on camera, on the school run and on the town.

171

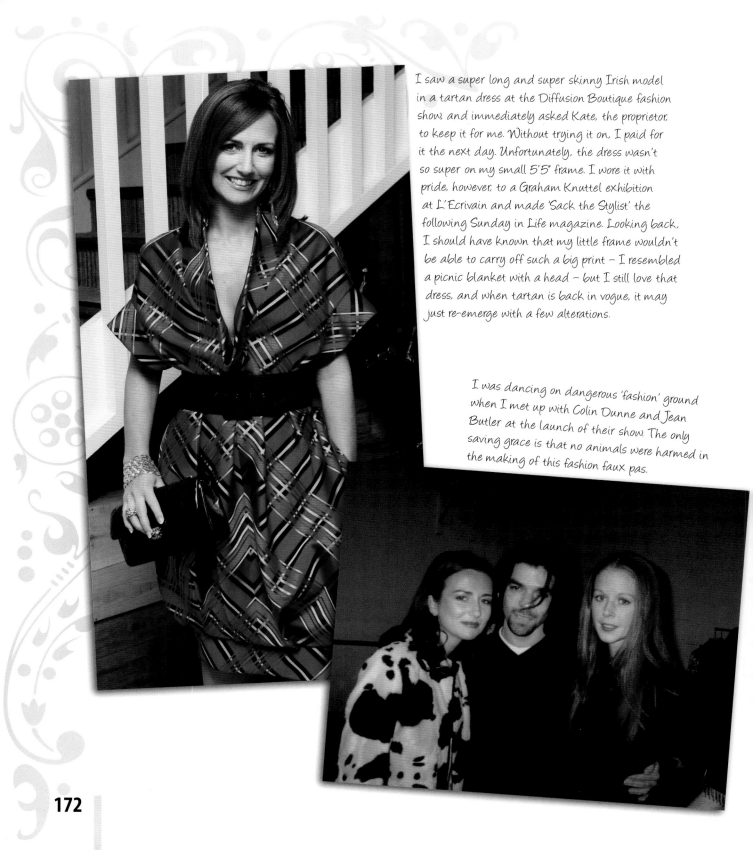

I saw a super long and super skinny Irish model in a tartan dress at the Diffusion Boutique fashion show, and immediately asked Kate, the proprietor, to keep it for me. Without trying it on, I paid for it the next day. Unfortunately, the dress wasn't so super on my small 5'5" frame. I wore it with pride, however, to a Graham Knuttel exhibition at L'Ecrivain and made 'Sack the Stylist' the following Sunday in Life magazine. Looking back, I should have known that my little frame wouldn't be able to carry off such a big print – I resembled a picnic blanket with a head – but I still love that dress, and when tartan is back in vogue, it may just re-emerge with a few alterations.

I was dancing on dangerous 'fashion' ground when I met up with Colin Dunne and Jean Butler at the launch of their show. The only saving grace is that no animals were harmed in the making of this fashion faux pas.

Another 'Sack the Stylist' moment.
I was papped leaving the Today FM
studios having done an interview with
Jenny, Mairead and Ray on the
Ray Darcy Show. It's funny, because
Ray Darcy had just enthused about
my cool jumpsuit on air. The jumpsuit
is from Divine Boutique, the belt is
Lara Bohinc from Seagreen, the bag
is Chesneau and the wedges are from
Havanna, Donnybrook.

Looking back, most of my wardrobe allowance in the early days of TV3 was spent in Karen Millen. Around the same time as Ireland's first commercial station was born, Karen Millen came to Ireland. As Entertainment and Fashion Correspondent, I needed a wardrobe and Karen needed a clotheshorse. You could argue that she got a bit of a Shetland pony with me, but her clothes just happened to naturally fit my shape very well. Unfortunately, TV3's budget didn't cover stylists, so it meant having to source my own wardrobe. I know what I like and what suits me, so I was very happy with this arrangement, especially since one of Karen's business partners in Ireland, Ian Galvin, who has incredible style, offered to assist me in creating a look for every season. Twice a year, Ian would close the shop at 6 o'clock and I would arrive in to try on the new season's collection. If Karen was in town, she would join us. I would try on clothes and shop for about two hours, and then we would all go out for a bite to eat. This relationship lasted for about four or five years, but as the Karen Millen label became more popular, more and more presenters were wearing it on television. Even within TV3 I would regularly discover that myself and another two or three presenters had the same dress. We would have a laugh about it, but I knew seeing a dress on the presenter on Ireland AM at 7 a.m. and then seeing the same dress on me at 6 p.m. would have looked as though we were all sharing the same wardrobe. Here I'm wearing Karen Millen to meet the President and the Taoiseach.

Wearing a Michelina Stacpoole dress and scarf (www.stacpoolekeane.com) and Chloe boots on the cover of the Irish Independent Life magazine.

No battle of the news anchors here – with TV pals Colette Fitzpatrick and Anne Doyle at the Irish Tatler Women of the Year Awards.

Hosting the TV Now Awards 2008 with Diarmuid Gavin. My dress is Deborah Veale and my jewellery is Lara Bohinc at Harvey Nichols.

Boilersuit chic! Wearing an Alexander McQueen jumpsuit and clutch and Buffalo shoes at the Harvey Nichols autumn/winter 2010 show.

At the Couples Retreat premiere. My entire outfit cost less than €100 from Zara. The shoes were around the same price from Buffalo.

Keeping it casual at the We Will Rock You premiere wearing a jacket from LA label BB Dakota, available from Irish website www.zuku.ie, and a Pauric Sweeney bag.

Fashionable fundraiser Adi Roche (one of my favourite ladies) at the Blue Haven Irish Showcase in Kinsale, Co. Cork. I'm wearing a Chanel jacket and Penneys pearls.

At the Coco Before Chanel premiere in another BB Dakota dress from www.zuku.ie with a bag from Louis Vuitton.

The Last Frame

Surprise, surprise, at a dinner party with Cilla Black.

One of my broadcasting heroes, Mr Gay Byrne. Always encouraging and complimentary, he really is the best in the business.

In good company as Bono and Dame Judi Dench are honoured by Trinity College.

Cate Blanchett flew to Dublin for the premiere of Veronica Guerin.

Academy Award winner Cuba Gooding, Jr.

Marvin Lee Aday, better known as Meatloaf, has sold an incredible 50 million albums.

Russell had just asked me if was I 'a bit leery'. Despite copious amounts of Pimm's, I did approach him with caution, but who could blame me? It was the pre-Wimbledon party in 2010 on the rooftop of Kensington Gardens. If you ask me, he's the one looking like a rabbit in the headlights.

Having a bad hair day with Tyra Banks.

Whoa! I've heard of being a crutch for someone, but being a table? It was a first for me, that's for sure, but I was happy to oblige and help Elle help Brown Thomas raise funds for Fashion Targets Breast Cancer.

After the interview, Phil Collins serenaded me at the piano.

Backstage at U2's Slane Castle concert with Charlize Theron.

Keeping it simple with Derry Clarke at the launch of his second cookbook in L'Ecrivain.

Sir Bob, a national treasure!

Ronnie Drew, we love you...

Star of The Truman Show, Ronin and Californication, Natascha McElhone was promoting the sci-fi film Solaris when I met her.

With Stephen Rea.

Looks like I'm trying to take Jim Corr's place.

Emma 'Baby Spice' Bunton.

Liam Neeson, a true gentleman.

Eddie Jordan started out working for Bank of Ireland, but ended up giving Michael Schumacher his first Formula One drive. Despite my appeals that the bank really needs him back, he seems content to continue with a career that is as successful as it is diverse.

It was a pleasure meeting Julianne Moore, who has starred in many of my favourite films (The Big Lebowski, Boogie Nights, The End of the Affair, Short Cuts and The Hand That Rocks the Cradle).

I love Graham Knuttel's artwork and have been a friend and collector of his for a long time.

Unique in every sense of the word, Guggi is one of my favourite artists and also one of my favourite people.

We have been lucky enough to see art superstar Gottfried Helnwein at work in his castle in Tipperary and pictured here in his studio in LA.

Artist Rasher's (aka Mark Kavanagh) first TV appearance was with me on Ireland AM. We have been great pals ever since.

Nothing scary about Mel B.

Adam Duritz (Counting Crows) was dating Courtney Cox when we met. Unfortunately, she didn't join him in Dublin.

At dinner with Tommy Hilfiger and his wife, Dee Ocleppo.

With Golden Globe, Screen Actors Guild and Emmy Award-winner Julianna Marguiles (ER, The Good Wife).

Wearing one of my Stacpoole & Keane dresses at a post-Grand Prix party in Monaco, with Formula 1 driver Heinz Harald Frentzen.

I enjoyed chatting with children from the Amazon School in Insinza, Zimbabwe, where Trócaires Global Gift Plan provides them with their only meal of the day.

Playing with pupils from second class at the Amazon School in Insinza, Zimbabwe, where Trocaire provides Global Gift lunches

With Ntokozi Maphosa at the Amazon School in Insinza, Zimbabwe, where Trócaire provides Global Gift school lunches.

In 2009, I finally had the time to do something _____ 'bout doing since I was a little girl – I travelled to Zimbabwe and Mozambique on a fundraising _____ aire. Without doubt it was the toughest, most emotional and most rewarding time in my life. I di_____ s from Africa to Ireland on radio and also produced my first mini TV documentary for Nationwia_____ e I was there. I saw first hand how Trócaire save lives every day in the poorest countries. If you would _____ 01 629 3333 or log on to www.trocaire.org.